Fresh From Dover Canyon

To Goeli + Josh —
Thanks for the great
olive oil! Best wishes
for a prosperous
(well-oiled =) future!
Mary Baker

Fresh From Dover Canyon

◆

Easy, Elegant Recipes from Dover Canyon Winery

Mary C Baker

iUniverse, Inc.
New York Lincoln Shanghai

Fresh From Dover Canyon
Easy, Elegant Recipes from Dover Canyon Winery

iUniverse, Inc.

For information address:
iUniverse, Inc.
2021 Pine Lake Road, Suite 100
Lincoln, NE 68512
www.iuniverse.com

ISBN: 0-595-29958-X

Printed in the United States of America

Contents

Simple Starters

Salads

Seafood

On the Grill

The Harvest Kitchen

Fresh from the Garden

Salsas and Sauces

Brunch Ideas

Just Desserts

Introduction

Fresh from Dover Canyon is a collection of favorite dishes that we prepare at our winery, Dover Canyon. Our focus is on fresh produce, herbs, and simple preparation. Our goal is to make it easy and fun to prepare an elegant meal. Some recipes are original, some are our own adaptations of popular dishes, and some are simple classics that we love.

Dover Canyon is a small winery in Paso Robles, California, perched on a windy hilltop with a view of rolling hills covered with pin oaks and bay. In addition to the winery barn and 1921 farmhouse, we have five acres of English walnuts, a seven-acre vineyard, and our organic garden beds. The winery is open on weekends for tasting, and our wine bar is in the cellar, snuggled right up to the barrels.

Paso Robles is the third largest wine appellation in California, so much of it is still open ranchland, populated with redtail hawks, boar, bobcats, cougars, deer, and black bear. Our winery is near the village of Templeton, where cars pause on Main Street to let wild turkeys cross the street. A leisurely exploration down historic Vineyard Drive will bring you past an herb farm, walnut, apple, and almond orchards, vineyards, a flower farm, and olive groves where vintage-pressed olive oil is produced.

We celebrate life in the winery and vineyard with easy recipes that rely on quality ingredients and fresh produce. If you're like us, you love to cook, but don't have time to make béchamel sauces or track down esoteric South American ingredients.

When you have a large family—or a lot of surprise visitors—it's helpful to have a repertoire of easy meals and versatile recipes, a well-stocked pantry, and access to a garden or a farmers' market. Therefore, *Fresh from Dover Canyon* includes easy-to-prepare, classic dishes that utilize fresh ingredients at hand, along with a list of pantry staples that we always rely on, and our favorite all-purpose herbs.

Our lifestyle is dedicated to hands-on, artisanal wine production. That means sixteen-hour days during harvest. Therefore, when we cook or grill, we have a deep fascination with robust flavors and fresh ingredients. Something fabulous and fast. We're hungry, hot, and tired, and we quite often have unexpected yet welcome guests, so we rely on our local sources of seafood and abalone, chicken, asparagus, nuts, salad greens, arugula and basil, stone fruits and citrus.

We like dishes that are rich in flavor, color, and aroma—dishes which are so easy and enjoyable to prepare that one can leisurely chop the garlic, warm the olive oil, roast peppers, sip a glass of wine, and still have dinner made in half an hour.

Fresh herbs, heirloom tomatoes, sweet peppers, hot peppers, and baby greens are packed with flavor and color. There's a lot of *wow* factor in dishes that use crunch, flavor, and color to good effect. In our gardens, we nurture fresh herbs, which are used for color, texture, and aroma as well as flavor; old-fashioned cultivars and heirloom plants; and a cornucopia of salad greens and baby root vegetables.

Our garden emphasizes vegetables and herbs which are expensive or hard to find in local markets. For instance, garlic is abundant in California, so we do not devote space in our tiny raised beds to the bulb. Instead, we plant fresh lettuces, exotic peppers, heirloom tomatoes, and different types of basil. Half-barrels filled with rosemary, oregano, thyme, and chives lie just outside the kitchen door.

We devote an entire raised bed to salad greens each spring and summer, planting a variety of mesclun greens, spinach, lettuces, and arugula in successive plantings every few weeks. Combinations of red and green lettuce and small bunches of spicy greens like arugula and watercress keep us supplied with greens, spring through fall. Fresh, flavorful greens require very little dressing. In fact, as you begin to discover the distinctive and sometimes very spicy flavors of locally grown salad greens, we think you'll begin to rely less on prepared salad dressings, which can seem very heavy-handed, and start making your own simple vinaigrettes of high quality olive oil and balsamic vinegar.

If you don't have time or space for a garden, we encourage you to try the mesclun mixes available in your supermarket, along with fresh herbs, baby vegetables, and seasonal produce readily available in stores and farmers' markets.

The Dover Canyon Kitchen

During our harvest season, which begins in early September and extends into November, we are hit with a double-whammy—no time and lots of visitors.

Harvest, or *crush* as it's referred to in the wine industry, involves long hours. Working sixteen hours a day for ten days straight is not uncommon. When fruit is ripening all at once, the hours can be even longer, and the weather can be brutal.

One chilly October night we finished cleaning the press at one o'clock in the morning. Frozen to the bone, exhausted, and hungry, we went home and made an omelette, because it was the only thing we could think of that would be fresh, hot, and ready in ten minutes. We kicked off our boots and fell asleep on our sofas in front of a roaring fire, fully clothed.

Whether you're a stock broker, a software engineer, or a vineyard owner, we all experience seasons of stress and effort that can be invigorating, but also exhausting. Getting together with friends is a gentle respite from pressure—but who wants to spend that rare free afternoon running around town collecting groceries and supplies, and then preparing an elaborate and time-consuming meal?

Not me!

A well-stocked pantry makes preparing impromptu dinners much easier. In fact, quite a few of our favorite classic, one-dish meals call for basic ingredients like chicken broth or chopped tomatoes.

Here are some good pantry basics for fresh, quick dishes. If you stock your cupboards with these items, you will always be able to concoct a delicious meal with any simple cut of meat and a handful of vegetables.

Chicken broth
Canned chopped tomatoes
Sea salt
Black peppercorns
Garlic bulbs
Olive oil
Balsamic vinegar

Canned black beans
Canned baby corn
Canned artichoke hearts
White or jasmine rice
Arborio rice
Penne, linguine and rigatoni pastas
Mongolian Fire Oil (chili oil)
Lemon pepper
Bread crumbs
Sun-dried tomatoes
Hoisin sauce
Sesame oil
Red pepper flakes
Worcestershire sauce
White Worcestershire sauce

How to Cook Without a Plan

I didn't learn to cook creatively until I was thirty-four years old. I thought all dishes worth eating were dictated by well-researched recipes that should be meticulously followed. I was never successful at doing that, and the results were often disastrous.

I learned lasagna, Parmesan popcorn, and Coq au Vin. That was my entire repertoire.

After I moved to Paso Robles and became involved in the wine community, I found myself backstage at winemaker dinners, watching chefs prepare gorgeous multi-course meals for dozens of people, while I polished glassware and fumbled with seating arrangements. The most amazing thing to me was that these nationally renowned chefs loved to talk about what they were doing, and were generous with descriptions of their techniques and plans. I was timid at first about asking questions, because the kitchens were always a hotbed of energized motion, raised voices, and undelivered ingredients. But what appeared to be panic in the kitchen is actually the accustomed pace of professional chefs and their staffs, so they were very tolerant of the little hospitality jock underfoot asking questions.

The most important thing I learned from pestering professional chefs is that proficiency in the kitchen is like a good wardrobe—if you have the basics, everything else is just color and fun.

Dan and I have certain basic dishes that we always fall back on when we're tired, feeling unimaginative, or scrounging in the bottom of the crisper. Risotto, pasta and bruschetta sauces are our diehard favorites.

RISOTTO

We love risotto for nights when we need something healthy, satisfying and comforting. Once you've made a basic risotto successfully, you will never need to look at a recipe again. The technique is simple and ingredients can be scavenged from the garden or vegetable crisper. We've included a basic recipe for risotto, but we also want to share a few simple tips for making risotto the Dover Canyon way.

Risotto is an Italian rice dish made by slowly stirring hot chicken, beef, or vegetable stock into rice, generally the small, round arborio rice. The result is a creamy, soul-satisfying glop to which you will add *condimenti*—vegetables, herbs, and possibly cream or cheese.

Browning the rice

Toss a cup of risotto rice into a large frypan and toast over medium heat until light brown. This gives the end result a richer flavor and a nice toasted color. Browning also seals the exterior of the rice, which helps it to absorb broth without losing texture.

Cooking slowly

This is not a dish for the impatient. Rushing the cooking process results in tough, crunchy, basically very nasty risotto. This is for evenings when you still have an hour of work on the computer, and your domestic associate wants a hot bath before dinner. It takes 45-60 minutes to make risotto, although the actual cooking time for the rice is 20-30 minutes. You'll want to give yourself a little more time for dicing, sautéing, and enjoying a glass of wine.

After the rice is browned, set it aside and sauté white onions, garlic, or a mirapoix in olive oil. If you have time to caramelize the onions, the resulting risotto will taste like candy for grownups. Add the browned rice back into the deliciously melted vegetables, and then begin adding broth, a cup or so at a time. It's a myth that you have to stir it every minute, but because the rice does absorb broth quickly, you need to check it every 5-10 minutes.

Leave out the cream

Many risotto recipes call for the addition of rich cream and cheese at the end. Who needs it? A pearly rice infused with chicken broth and melded with onions, peppers, seafood, and sausage doesn't really need anything else. This is why it's important to toast the rice and patiently caramelize onions or sauté garlic before starting the simmer. The resulting flavors are rich and satisfying.

Experiment with vegetables and seafood

Risotto is a great dish for that bottom-of-the-vegetable-crisper night. We've used green and yellow squash, every color of sweet pepper, sausage, shrimp, scallops, white onions, garlic, broccoli, leeks, and spinach. Chicken and sausage should be cooked or sautéed ahead of time and added toward the end, along with fresh vegetables. It's fun to play with combinations, and some ingredients do beg for just a little Parmesan-Reggiano at the end. However, risotto is not a dish to wait patiently on the shelf until you have just the "right" ingredients, so pull out that arborio rice whenever you want a warm, satisfying meal.

PASTA

Pasta is a staple in our household. How can you not have a whole shelf devoted to good semolina pasta? It's quick and easy, can be topped with anything, packed in a tub for the kids' school lunch, makes an instant midnight snack, doesn't smash the other groceries in your bag, doesn't have an expiration date, and is really, really cheap.

We have our own way of doing pasta. We like it fresh, hot and relatively undisguised by sauce. Sauce and toppings are important, but a well-cooked pasta is such a soul-satisfying art food (look at all the shapes!) that we like the pasta to be as important as the other ingredients.

Don't overcook

First of all, it's way too easy to overcook pasta. Eight to twelve minutes is adequate for even the heaviest cut of pasta. When you remove pasta from the stove, do not let it sit in its cooking water; drain it immediately or it will continue to cook in its retained heat and turn mushy while your back is turned.

The rinsing dilemma

As a youngster, I always heard that you should rinse away the "starch" with cold water. Several decades later, someone pointed out to me that pasta *is* starch. If you're going to eat pasta, why are you washing away a little starch dust with chilled water that makes your pasta cold? Now that I'm grown up, I completely ignore that advice. I like my pasta hot.

However, if you're going to make a cold pasta *salad*, or if you need to set the pasta aside while preparing other dishes, then it does become important to rinse the pasta in cold water. If you dump it into a bowl or colander while it's still hot, it will continue to cook in its own retained heat and become limp and over-cooked. If you've inadvertently cooked it a little too long, throw some ice cubes in the strainer as well, and attempt a cryogenic halt.

Heating plates

If the pasta is done but you're not ready to serve it, warm your dinner plates in the oven or microwave. (Oven heat is retained longer.) If your pasta is lukewarm, that's okay—just spoon it onto a warm plate, make sure your sauce is hot when you spoon it over, and it will taste delicious.

Don't mix the noodles and sauce

One night in the middle of crush, with lots of people hanging around "helping," Dan endeavored to make linguine, and a pasta sauce of sausage, tomatoes and herbs for our crowd of onlookers. In the meantime, he was also operating the forklift, crusher, and press, and trying to keep his five-year-old son from climbing up on the equipment and getting chopped to pieces.

The kitchen smelled great. He had sautéed onions, peppers, and garlic, added fresh chopped tomatoes from the garden, and some high-quality sausage. The linguine was done, rinsed, and set to the side. His sauce was quietly simmering, waiting for an auspicious dinnertime. However, a guest decided that Dan had too much to do, and she took matters into her own hands. She dumped the linguine into the sauce, stirred it thoroughly, turned off the heat and left it. By the time we paused for dinner at ten o'clock that night, Dan's delicate linguine was mush and the pasta sauce tasted like cereal.

Pasta is beautifully versatile and very forgiving of schedules, if you allow it to be itself. Keep the pasta separate. Spoon it artistically onto a dinner plate. Cover it with a rich, aromatic sauce. Give your guests a rotary grater filled with hard Parmesan cheese, and offer a small bowl of fresh, shredded basil leaves.

BRUSCHETTA

We call this freeform version of garlic-infused olive oil *bruschetta* (pronounced broosh-ket-ta) only because we don't know of any other Italian term that really describes it. Traditionally, bruschetta is an olive oil, tomato, and garlic condiment served on slices of toasted baguette. We've taken it beyond the traditional parameters by throwing in whatever our garden gods bestow upon us—broccoli, yellow fingerling squash, tomatoes, asparagus, and herbs.

The beauty of this combination, aside from crisper-raiding possibilities, is rich aroma, colorful presentation, and versatility. Basically, you're just sautéing vegetables in olive oil and garlic. Bruschetta can be served over meat, potatoes, pasta, eggs or even toast.

Don't get the oil too hot

Never get impatient with olive oil. The idea is to let flavors infuse into the oil, not to force the oil to cook other ingredients. Warm the olive oil and garlic over very low heat while chopping other ingredients. Olive oil is surprisingly seductive. Even if you forget to turn on the stove at all, it will still absorb some of the flavor of your garlic or herbs.

Don't burn the garlic

Garlic turns sweet and soft as it's sautéed or baked, but when pieces of garlic turn brown, they shrink and become tough and bitter. If you're sautéing chopped garlic in olive oil, err on the safe side and keep the heat very low, or even off. It doesn't take long to sauté small pieces of garlic. If you need to leave the room, move the pan away from the heat until you return. Warm olive oil will continue coaxing out that garlic flavor without a lot of effort.

Chop the vegetables you've chosen into small, bite-size pieces, and add them to the oil just five to ten minutes before you are ready to eat. Mushrooms can be added early—they will absorb some of the cooking oil, but then release oil and moisture as they soften.

Stir everything attentively and sauté until all the vegetables are soft, but still brightly-colored.

Put tomatoes in last and just heat through

Roma tomatoes are the best choice for a bruschetta-style sauté. Other tomatoes are too juicy and release copious quantities of watery juice into your bruschetta. Think of serving hot, tomato-flavored water over your pasta and you'll get the idea. Romas are a mealy, thick-skinned tomato bred for making tomato paste, which makes them perfect for a quick sauté. If you would like to use heirloom tomatoes, cut them in half first and scoop out any soft interior and excess juice. Cut the tomatoes into small, bite-size chunks and throw them in at the very end of your sauté. Heat through quickly (even romas release some juice) and serve your bruschetta immediately.

The American Way: Notes on Wine

The wine pairing suggestions in this cookbook are references to varietals like cabernet, chardonnay, pinot noir, and zinfandel, with a few adventurous references to grapes like sangiovese and viognier. I think it's always easiest to begin with the familiar and explore outward from there. There's no need to stay on this continent, however. I encourage you to poke around your local wine store, ask a lot of annoying questions, and bring home some intercontinental selections like a Pouilly-Fuissé or a Gigondas.

In Europe, wines are named for the region in which they are grown. The concept of *terroir*, which is the effect of soil and climate on the crops of a region, is important in the traditions of viticulture and winemaking. European wines are sometimes a complete varietal, but more often they are blends that feature the predominant characteristics of a region, like the luscious, smoky Côtes-du-Rhône blends of syrah, grenache, and mourvedre, or Chianti Classicos, which are Italian blends of sangiovese, trebbiano, dolcetto, and other regional varieties.

In America, our hereditary fascination with wine was disrupted by World Wars, Prohibition, and the Great Depression, and has only recently regained ground in the last few decades. In the meantime, our vinous recovery has been affected by my generation's exposure to television advertising's "100% new and improved" concept, which suggests that a wine must be one hundred percent varietal and one hundred percent estate grown. Tasting a one-hundred-percent wine is a great way to learn about basic wine varietals—Cabernet, for instance, has a core flavor of black cherry with elements of cinnamon, licorice, or herb depending on where it's grown, while Pinot Noir has a core flavor of tart pie cherry with elements of mushroom, compost, and herbs. It's also easier to compare one region against another if you're cross-tasting with a single varietal.

But for sheer food-friendliness, a blend can't be beat. Think of it this way: would you make a pasta sauce out of one-hundred-percent tomatoes? No herbs, no garlic? In cooking, as in wine, it's important to savor the elemental flavor of a single, carefully produced food, but there are also moments when ultimate satisfaction comes from carefully blended components creating a beautiful synchronicity of aroma, color, and flavor.

Pairing Wine and Food

Wines are generally paired with food around two criteria—weight and flavor. It sounds odd at first to think of wine as having weight, but wine does have a certain heft on the palate. Some of that heft is due to tannic structure—cabernets and syrahs, for instance, have plenty of tannin, while pinot noirs are generally lighter. A wine's weight also depends on its alcohol content. Higher levels of alcohol give wine a thicker mouthfeel. Wines with a higher alcohol content cling to the glass more, having thicker *legs*, and considerably more weight on the palate. Swirled water, for instance, has no legs—but swirled brandy has drips like cake frosting.

To choose a wine for a particular dish or meal, I consider the weight of the food before anything else. If it's light fare, such as heirloom tomatoes, light pasta dishes, salad, or pale meats, I would choose from a spectrum of wines that might include whites and light-bodied reds. If a dish involves red meat, heavy sauces, and comforting carbohydrates like mashed potatoes, I would gravitate toward heavier reds like cabernet, syrah, and zinfandel.

The second pairing criterion is flavor. I try to match dishes with wines that have similar flavors. The tricky thing is to look for flavors that are really evident in the dish, because sauces, grilling, and herbs will affect the overall flavor and feel of a dish. For instance, we like to grill racks of baby New Zealand lamb, rubbed with sea salt, coarsely ground black pepper, and herbs de Provence. Lamb is generally considered a light meat, but the pepper, lavender, and other herbs in the rub give it an incense-like finish, and barbecuing imparts a light char. Therefore, syrah and zinfandel are good matches for an otherwise feminine cut of meat. An otherwise light vegetarian pasta that is heavily laden with garlic, roasted tomatoes, peppers, or caramelized onions would be better with a sangiovese or zinfandel than a crisp white wine.

To add to the confusion, basic wine varietals like chardonnay, cabernet, syrah, and zinfandel are huge categories with myriad variations. You can taste a thousand chardonnays and find flavors ranging from light, crisp, pear flavors to heavy butterscotch. Red wines offer flavors starting at strawberry and working their way toward road tar.

Pairing wine and food should be fun and adventurous, however—not some demented adult game of Memory Match. Relax, explore, and learn. Invite your guests to bring wines or make suggestions. Cook what you like, and open a range of wines for your guests. For instance, if you're serving grilled prawns as an appetizer, steak and vegetables for dinner, and a cheese plate for fireside chat, then open a sauvignon blanc or chardonnay, a pinot noir, a cabernet, and maybe a Late Harvest zinfandel. Leftover wine? No problem—get a metallic pen, have everybody write merry signatures on the bottles, and send the wine home with your guests.

WINE GLASSES

If you plan to serve several wines during a multi-course meal, have enough glasses on hand so that diners can finish each wine at their leisure. If you plan on serving a white, a red, and a dessert wine, try to provide three appropriate glasses for each guest. That way, if a guest loves the white wine but is not sure about reds, she can continue to linger with the white wine into the next course. You can pour two to three ounces of red wine in the second glass for her to try when she is ready.

If you're dining outside and the weather is hot, keep the glasses in a cool, shady place until shortly before dining. If you set the glasses out too early they will get hot, which will have an unpleasant effect on your guests' wine enjoyment.

THE BIG CHILL

Chilling reduces the movement of volatile molecules in wine. In other words, it suppresses aroma and flavor temporarily. Also, the shock of a chilled beverage hitting the palate closes your senses to flavors. If you want a wine to show at it's best, it should be about 50-52° when you serve it. If the bottle feels very cool to your palm, the temperature is perfect.

However, if it's 80° outside and you take your bottle of fine red wine directly out to the table, it's going to quickly become warm. Very warm. Therefore, it's perfectly all right to chill wines, both white and red, when you plan to dine outside in warm weather.

Do not put them in the freezer, exactly—just simulate the effect of cellar storage by laying the bottles on their side for a while in the refrigerator. The warmer the weather, the colder the bottles can be. While you don't necessarily want to chill a fine red wine, putting the bottles in the refrigerator for only a half hour or so will really chill only the bottle itself; it takes longer than that for the temperature of the wine to drop. And chilling the bottle a little will insulate the wine inside against your warm al fresco setting.

When the wine is served into glasses, each glass will warm up quickly, so keep that in mind, and pour only four ounces of wine at a time, keeping the wine bottle in a cool, shady spot. Personally, I feel it's better to err a little on the cold side than the warm side if the weather is hot.

Simple Starters

Brie and Basil Crostini

Crostini are a simple, classic starter for entertaining.

1 thin sourdough baguette, sliced
1/4 cup olive oil
3 cloves garlic, peeled and pressed
8 oz. Brie or Camembert
1 handful fresh basil leaves, destemmed

Makes about 24 crostini

Warm the garlic in olive oil in a small basting pan. Brush over both sides of the baguette slices and toast very lightly under the broiler, about 12" away from the heat, checking frequently and turning to toast both sides. Remove and place one basil leaf on each slice, covering with a slice of cheese. Return to the oven and broil until the cheese is melted, 2-3 minutes. Remove and allow to cool. Garnish some of the crostini with tiny basil leaves tucked into the molten cheese.

Smoked Salmon Crostini

1 thin sourdough baguette, sliced
1/4 cup olive oil
3 cloves garlic, peeled and pressed
8 oz. fresh or smoked salmon
4 oz. cream cheese
3 tablespoons fresh dill, chopped
1/4 cup sour cream
2 tablespoons milk

Makes about 24 crostini

Warm the garlic in olive oil in a small basting pan. Brush over both sides of the baguette slices and toast very lightly under the broiler, about 12" away from the heat, checking frequently and turning to toast both sides.

In a blender, pulse the salmon, cream cheese, sour cream, and dill until thick and creamy. If the mixture is too thick, add a spoonful of milk until it becomes easy to spread.

Spread the salmon mixture generously over the toasted baguettes, garnishing with tiny leaves of dill.

Pastry Wedges with Nectarine~Ginger Relish

1 package prepared pie crust (2 crusts)
1 egg, beaten until frothy
4 fresh nectarines, pitted and finely chopped
2 tablespoons Tequila or rum
2 tablespoons grated fresh ginger root
4-5 green onions, chopped fine

Makes 16 pastry wedges

In a medium bowl, combine the liquor and ginger, and let the mixture steep for at least five minutes. Add the chopped nectarines and onions, and stir.

Unroll the prepared pastry and brush lightly with beaten egg. Cut each round into eight wedges and place on a non-stick cookie sheet. Bake in a 400° oven for about ten minutes, until lightly browned and crisp. Allow to cool. Place a spoonful of nectarine relish on each wedge, and serve. Leftover nectarine relish can be placed in a small serving bowl for extra dips.

Wine suggestion:

For the crostini, a slightly chilled white of any style. Sauvignon blanc, pinot blanc, chardonnay or viognier would all work well. For the wedges, which are slightly spicy from the ginger, I suggest a sparkling white like a brut champagne.

Salads

Golden Gazpacho

A crunchy chilled dish of yellow pear tomatoes, sweet yellow peppers, garlic, and bits of red bell pepper, combined with traditional ingredients like cucumber, onion, and cilantro.

Gazpacho is usually a chilled dish made of pureed or processed fruits and vegetables. We prefer to make ours thick and chunky, with plenty of garlic. This brightly colored and flavorful gazpacho is a refreshing side dish with red meat and potatoes.

2 cups yellow pear tomatoes, sliced in half
2 yellow bell pepper, seeds removed and diced
1 red bell pepper, seeds removed and diced
1 cucumber, peeled, seeds removed and diced
1 bunch green onions, chopped
3 garlic cloves, finely chopped
1 bunch cilantro, destemmed and finely chopped
1 jalapeno, seeds removed and diced
2/3 cup olive oil
3 tablespoons white wine vinegar
3 tablespoons finely chopped fresh herbs—chives, oregano, or thyme
Sea salt and coarsely ground pepper

Serves 4-6

Combine the chopped tomatoes, peppers, cucumbers, onions, garlic, cilantro and jalapeno in a large bowl. In a small bowl, make a vinaigrette by combining the olive oil, white wine vinegar, and herbs. Taste the vinaigrette and add salt and pepper to taste.
Toss the gazpacho with the vinaigrette and let it sit for several hours if possible so the garlic can permeate the olive oil and chopped vegetables. Serve chilled.

Wine suggestion:

A crisp, chilled sauvignon blanc or pinot gris.

Prawn Gazpacho

Pickled tiger prawns combined in a chunky garlic gazpacho.
This is a great item for winery and concert picnics. It keeps well, travels well, and if you bring extra bowls and spoons, you'll make lots of new friends.

My original recipe was published by Bon Appetit in the April 1992 issue, then again in their 20-Minute Special Edition issue, and included again in the 1992 hardbound collector's edition. The recipe was altered by the editors to be more like a traditional gazpacho, including the incorporation of four cups of tomato juice. But this is the original crunchy, fresh-from-the-garden, high garlic, many-prawns version.

1 pound of large tiger shrimp or prawns, peeled
6 garlic cloves, chopped
2 tablespoons red wine vinegar
Juice of 1 lemon

12 roma tomatoes
1/4 cup olive oil
1 green bell pepper, chopped
1 yellow bell pepper, chopped
1 cucumber, peeled, seeds removed, chopped
1 bunch green onions, chopped
3 jalapenos, seeds removed and minced
1 bunch fresh cilantro, chopped, reserving some for garnish
1 lemon, cut into wedges for garnish

Serves 6-8

Marinate the prawns and garlic in the vinegar and lemon juice for 1 to 2 hours, or overnight. If you feel more comfortable with cooked seafood, sauté the prawns in a spoonful of olive oil until barely bright pink, and cool.

Combine all ingredients, including prawns and marinade. Season with salt and coarsely ground pepper.

To serve, ladle the gazpacho into small cups or bowls. Garnish with lemon wedges and fresh cilantro.

Wine suggestion:

A crisp, slightly acidic white with lots of fruit and delicate herbal notes. Good selections would be sauvignon blanc, malvasia bianca, or tank-fermented chardonnay.

Nancy's Salad

Ted and Nancy Commerdinger travel from southern California to Paso Robles on wine festival weekends to pour wine and help with sales at Midnight Cellars. At the end of a long day, Nancy makes this salad for Bob Hartenberger at Midnight Cellars. He loves the simplicity, flavor, and soul-satisfying qualities of this crisp salad, especially when served with winemaker Rich Hartenberger's slow-cooked beef in reduced tomato sauce. Meanwhile, Ted Commerdinger would be preparing his Triple Threat Mashed Potatoes.

2 medium heads of Romaine lettuce, washed and patted dry
4 oz. pine nuts, lightly toasted
4 oz. feta cheese
Balsamic vinegar to taste
Freshly cracked black pepper
Cherry or pear tomatoes (optional)

Serves 4

Assemble three Romaine leaves in a fan on each salad plate. Distribute the feta and pine nuts randomly atop the leaves. Drizzle with balsamic vinegar and season with black pepper. Add tomatoes if in season.

Wine suggestion:

A crisp, chilled sauvignon blanc or pinot gris.

Seattle Salad with Raspberry-Sesame Vinaigrette

This salad is a Northwest-style combination of fresh greens and Pacific Rim flavors.

2 cups mixed greens
1/4 cup baby arugula
1 cup fresh pineapple, cut into ½" spears
1/4 red bell pepper, seeds removed, finely diced
1 tablespoon toasted sesame seeds, optional

Raspberry-Sesame Vinaigrette

2 tablespoons sesame oil
1 tablespoon olive oil, optional
1-2 tablespoons raspberry vinegar
1 teaspoon each chopped garlic chives and thyme
Salt and pepper to taste

Combine the salad greens and arugula in a colorful bowl or directly on serving plates. Sprinkle the pineapple chunks over the greens and top with sprinklings of red bell pepper and sesame seeds.

For the vinaigrette, combine the sesame oil, one tablespoon of the raspberry vinegar, and herbs. Whisk or stir, and taste. Sesame oils vary in quality and flavor—we prefer dark oils with a nutty, toasted flavor. Raspberry vinegars also vary in acetic quality—some taste slightly sweet, while others are more acidic but have stronger raspberry flavor. Adjust all quantities to your preference, and serve in a small vinaigrette carafe. A tiny drizzle on your salad will deliver a cargo of flavor.

Wine suggestion:

The tropical flavors of a chilled viognier or roussanne would complement spicy dishes like Prawns in Ginger-Peanut Sauce, and would be excellent served with this fruity, yet spicy, salad.

Corn, Bean and Cilantro Salad

A wild and wonderfully textured salad that is also chunky, hearty, and colorful, great with steaks or tritip.

2 12 oz. cans yellow corn niblets, drained and rinsed
    or 2-3 cups fire-roasted corn, cut from the cob
1 27 oz. can red kidney beans, drained and rinsed
1 12 oz. can black beans, drained and rinsed
1 red bell pepper, seeds removed and diced
1/2 cup toasted sunflower seeds
2 bunches green onions, chopped
1 bunch cilantro, destemmed and finely diced
1/2 cup Italian salad dressing, or olive oil and balsamic vinegar to taste

Serves 6-8

Combine the corn, beans, seeds and vegetables in an attractive bowl and chill. Gently toss with purchased or homemade dressing just before serving. The corn and beans will absorb dressing and become soggy, so always add the dressing just before serving, or serve the salad dressing separately in a bowl or carafe.

Wine suggestion:

Since this salad is excellent with a hearty cut of meat, try a pinot noir or sangiovese.

Field Greens with Roasted Baby Spring Vegies

You can get a jump start on spring in many areas by planting cold-hardy varieties of greens, peas, and root vegetables in fall or late winter. Use thinnings as baby greens in a delicious salad.

2 cups mixed greens (lettuces, arugula, watercress, baby spinach or pak choy greens)
1 cup mixed color cherry tomatoes, halved
1 cup sugar pod peas
1 tablespoon olive oil
1 clove garlic, pressed
1 handful baby carrots, trimmed and cleaned
1 cup baby beets, halved or quartered

Vinaigrette:

1/4 cup olive oil
1 tablespoon balsamic vinegar
1 tablespoon chopped fresh chives and tarragon
Sea salt and freshly cracked black pepper

Serves 4

Toss the greens, and sprinkle the cherry tomatoes and peas over the salad. Press the garlic into the olive oil, stir well, then baste the carrots and baby beets with the oil. Put the carrots and beets into separate foil or pie pans (to keep the beets from bleeding onto the carrots). You can also arrange them on a cookie sheet in two open envelopes of aluminum foil. Roast in the oven at 400° for about 20 minutes, turning halfway through, until the roots are browned. Allow to cool, or bring to room temperature quickly by setting them in the freezer, and add to the salad.

Whisk the vinaigrette ingredients together and drizzle over the salad.

Wine suggestion:

A buttery chardonnay, a pinot noir or a sangiovese.

Mesclun Salad with Raspberries and Black Pepper

Easy, impressive, and great with red meats.

1 bag fresh mesclun greens
1 cup fresh arugula, torn into small pieces
1/2 cup fresh, firm raspberries
1/4 cup pine nuts, lightly toasted

Dressing:

1/4 cup olive oil
1 tablespoon balsamic vinegar
1 tablespoon Bonny Doon's Framboise (raspberry dessert wine)
2 tablespoons combined fresh chives, oregano and tarragon
Coarsely ground black pepper, to taste

Serves 4

Place the pine nuts in a frying pan, without oil, and toast over medium heat until lightly browned. Set aside to cool. Combine salad ingredients, sprinkling pine nuts, raspberries, and pepper lightly over the salad just before serving.

Finely chop the herbs, combine dressing ingredients, and stir vigorously with a fork or whisk until the oil and vinegar are well combined. Pour lightly over the salad just before serving. Add pepper to taste.

Wine suggestion:

This salad is excellent with the Grilled Tritip in Late Harvest Zinfandel and Black Pepper Marinade, so serve up a dark, jammy zinfandel.

Dover Canyon Pasta Salad

This dish is a favorite among our friends. We use fresh tomatoes and basil from our own organic garden beds, and we serve dinner outside in the shade of 100-year-old walnut trees near the winery.

12-16 oz.(one package) rotelli or rotini pasta
   (Rotelli is more traditional, but we've also used penne and small rigatoni—
   anything with a twisted or tubular shape will collect delicious pockets of
   dressing and grated cheese.)
Dash of sea salt
2 cups red or yellow tomatoes, cubed
2 avocados, pitted and cubed, optional
1/2 cup basil leaves, torn into ½" pieces
4 oz. Reggiano/Parmesan cheese, coarsely grated
(We like Reggiano/Parmesan for this salad because it's slightly salty and adds a
lot of flavor, but you can substitute other hard cheeses as well.)
1/2 cup extra virgin olive oil
1 tablespoon balsamic vinegar
2 tablespoons fresh chopped herbs—oregano, chives, or basil
Sea salt and freshly cracked black pepper to taste

Serves 6-8

In a large stockpot, bring 8 cups of water and a dash of sea salt to a boil. Add the pasta and cook over medium heat according to package directions until al dente, 8 to 12 minutes. Remove from heat, rinse pasta with cold water and drain thoroughly. Allow to cool.

In a large, attractive bowl, gently combine the pasta, roma tomatoes, avocado, basil and grated Reggiano/Parmesan.

In a small bowl, whisk together the olive oil, balsamic vinegar and herbs. Pour over the pasta salad and toss gently. Cover with plastic wrap and allow to marinate in the refrigerator for at least half an hour. Toss again before serving.

Wine suggestion:

Anything from a chilled sauvignon blanc to a mellow white like chardonnay or pinot blanc, or gently spicy reds like pinot noir and sangiovese.

Red and Yellow Tomatoes with Mozzarella and Basil

Beautiful, fast, and aromatic, this salad plate is easy to make and impressive to serve. The tomatoes must be firm, large, and flavorful—we like to use heirloom tomatoes still warm from the garden.

3 or 4 red tomatoes
3 or 4 yellow tomatoes
1 8 oz. package Mozzarella cheese
1 tablespoon balsamic vinegar[1]
1/4 cup olive oil[1]
1 cup fresh basil leaves

Serves 4

Slice the tomatoes with a large, sharp knife (we use a serrated bread knife), into ½ inch thick slices and arrange in overlapping patterns on a colorful plate. Blue and green plates set off the tomato colors well.

Cut the Mozzarella into ½ inch cubes and sprinkle over the tomatoes. Drizzle olive oil and balsamic vinegar over the tomatoes and cheese. Wash and destem the basil leaves, tear into one-inch pieces, leaving small leaves whole, and sprinkle over the tomatoes and cheese.

Wine suggestion:

This salad can be served as a side dish—or as an aperitif plate with a crisp, dry white wine, like a young, vibrant viognier or roussanne. Other good selections would be sauvignon blanc or malvasia bianca.

---

1.   A really good balsamic vinegar will be soft and oaky—ripe tomatoes may not need anything else, so use olive oil only if you feel it will balance the vinegar.

Tomato, Sweet Pepper, and Basil Salad with Honey-Orange Dressing

A combination of sweet peppers and colorful cherry tomatoes, brought together in a sweet orange dressing. A sweet, crunchy, and colorful accompaniment to Thai Fire Chicken.

1 green bell pepper, seeds removed and coarsely chopped
1 yellow bell pepper, seeds removed and coarsely chopped
1 red bell pepper, seeds removed and coarsely chopped
1 exotic bell pepper (orange, chocolate, purple, etc.), seeds removed and coarsely chopped
1 small produce box (about 1 cup) of yellow cherry or pear tomatoes, halved
1 small produce box (about 1 cup) of red cherry tomatoes, halved
10-20 leaves of fresh basil, torn into slivers

Serves 4-6

Honey Orange Dressing

2 tablespoons honey
3 tablespoons rice vinegar or white wine
3 tablespoons olive oil
Juice of 1 large navel orange
Fresh tarragon, chives, or garlic chives, chopped
Salt and pepper to taste

Toss the salad ingredients together in a large, colorful bowl. Mix the dressing ingredients in a small bowl and whisk until thoroughly combined. Adjust the herbs, salt, and pepper to taste. Pour the dressing over the vegetables a little at a time, and toss until lightly coated.

Wine suggestion:

This salad is excellent with spicy chicken and fish dishes, so try a crisp, chilled white like sauvignon blanc, pinot gris or pinot blanc.

Seafood

Grilled Mahi Mahi with Yogurt Tartar

Simple, fast and impressive.

2 mahi mahi steaks, about 1" thick
Juice of 1 navel orange
1 tablespoon honey
3 tablespoons Mongolian Fire Oil (or any high-quality chili oil)
2 handfuls of fresh sage leaves, chopped fine
Black peppercorns, coarsely ground in a hand or coffee grinder

Serves 2

Yogurt Tartar

This side dish is based on the cooling yogurt dishes of East Indian cuisine. Serve a dollop to the side of the mahi mahi, to balance the heat of the chili oil and black peppercorns.

1 cup of unflavored, live culture yogurt
1/2 English or Armenian cucumber, peeled and chopped
1 tablespoon fresh mint, chopped
1 tablespoon of fresh chives, chopped
Sea salt and black pepper to taste

Get the barbecue really hot, then scoop the hottest coals to the outside of the grill, leaving the center medium-hot. Combine the orange juice, honey and chili oil in a small bowl; whisk thoroughly. If the ingredients do not combine well, the honey may be too cold. Warm the marinade over the grill or in the microwave and then whisk.

41

Rub the mahi mahi steaks with chopped sage and freshly ground pepper. Clean the grill well, and place the steaks over the center of the grill, basting with the marinade. Turn frequently with a large spatula, sprinkling with additional pepper each time. The honey seals in moisture and helps the pepper adhere to the fish. (If you're feeling confident, turn each steak 90° clockwise on each flip, for those cool cross-hatch grill marks.)

Cooking time should total about 5 minutes on each side, depending on the temperature of your grill, and the thickness of the steaks. High heat will grill the outside faster than the inside. A little more patience and medium heat will give you a steak heated thoroughly through. If you're not sure, err on the conservative side, as fish is easily overcooked. You can always send it back to the grill for a few minutes. Cook the steaks until they begin to flake, but are still juicy and translucent inside, then remove to a platter.

Mix the tartar ingredients together and serve on the side as a condiment with the mahi mahi. (The more chili oil and pepper you use, the more your guests will appreciate the cooling influence of the yogurt.)

Wine suggestion:

The slightly hot and pungent flavors of the fire oil and fresh sage call for a red wine with plenty of grip and spice, like sangiovese or zinfandel.

Lobster, Mesclun and Arugula Salad

This is an extremely elegant dish, fresh and light, yet surprisingly rich.

1 fresh lobster for every two people
2 handfuls of baby mesclun greens for each person
1 handful of arugula for each person
1 avocado for every 2 people

Dressing
(For six people)
5 tablespoons olive oil
3 tablespoons of a fine white wine
3 tablespoons stone ground mustard

Serves 6

At least 2 hours before dinner boil the lobsters, drain and chill. Better yet, have them boiled for you at your local market.

Toss the greens together and arrange a fluffy bed on each salad plate.

Split the lobster tails lengthwise into two long sections each, and place one section in the center of each salad. Arrange claw meat around the tail piece. We have a talented friend who can extract the claw meat in one piece so that when we place it on the plate it still looks like a claw. But if the claw meat shreds when you pull it out, just sprinkle it over the greens.

Peel, pit, and slice the avocado, arranging slices over the salad.

Whisk together the dressing ingredients and drizzle over the salad.

Wine suggestion:

A chilled viognier.

Lemon-Infused Salmon Filet with Dill and Capers

Salmon steamed on the grill with lemon slices, fresh dill, and capers. Fast, easy and elegant.

1 large salmon filet for every 4 people
1 lemon
1 handful of dill sprigs
2 tablespoons capers (optional)

Serves 4

Spread out two layers of aluminum foil, large enough to wrap amply around the filet.
Rub the foil lightly with olive oil. Lay the filet on the foil, skin side down. Slice the lemon thinly and overlap the slices in a row on the filet. Lay several sprigs of fresh dill on top of the lemon. Sprinkle a handful of capers over everything. Wrap the filet in the foil, tightly sealing the ends.

Grill over medium heat for 10-15 minutes. Remove from heat and allow to sit for another 10-15 minutes. The salmon will continue to steam in its foil pouch.

Slice the filet into servings and garnish with fresh dill and capers.

Wine suggestion:

We like to serve the salmon with our Peach-Ginger Salsa. The salsa is fruity but the ginger and Hungarian wax peppers also make it hot, so we recommend serving a chilled viognier or off-dry riesling.

Peach-Ginger Salsa

A spicy condiment that goes well with salmon, chicken, and other light meats. The Tequila gives it a nutty flavor and quickly extracts heat and flavor from the other ingredients.

4 fresh peaches, or one 16 oz. can of cling peaches, chopped
2 tablespoons Tequila
2 cloves garlic, chopped fine or pressed
2 tablespoons grated fresh ginger root
1 yellow Hungarian wax pepper, seeds removed and chopped fine
4-5 green onions, chopped fine
1/2 bunch cilantro, chopped

Makes about 1 pint

Put the chopped peaches in a small serving bowl. In another small bowl or cup, combine the Tequila, garlic, ginger and pepper, and let the mixture steep for at least five minutes. The alcohol extracts flavor and heat from the garlic, ginger, and pepper, so the longer you let it steep, the "hotter" your fruit salsa will be. Combine all ingredients with the peaches and serve.

Bouillabaisse with Saffron and Leeks

Fast and easy—a few threads of saffron give it a deep golden color and exotic flavor.

1/4 cup olive oil
2 cups mirapoix:
    3 medium carrots, diced
    1 white onion, diced
    2 stalks celery, diced
1 leek
3 cloves garlic, chopped
2" fresh ginger root, peeled and grated
Sea salt and coarsely ground black pepper, to taste
4 cups chicken broth
1 cup clam broth
1 cup white wine
Saffron, a tiny pinch (available from Penzey's Spices)
2 tablespoons fresh chopped herbs, optional—tarragon, chives, or thyme
2-3 pounds mixed shellfish—clams, mussels, prawns, crab legs and claws
1-2 pounds mixed seafood—scallops, salmon, squid, cod, halibut, etc., cut into 2-3" pieces

Serves 4 (or Dan and Mary)

In a ten-quart pot, warm the olive oil and add the mirapoix. Sauté over medium-low heat until the vegetables are soft and aromatic, about 5 minutes. Meanwhile, pull the leek's outer leaves apart slightly, and cut a 1/4" groove down its length. Rinse the leek thoroughly, as sand tends to collect inside them. Drain and slice, discarding the green ends. Add the leek, garlic, and ginger to the olive oil and stir until delicately translucent. Taste the sautéed mixture and add salt and pepper to taste. Add the chicken and clam broth, wine, two or three threads of saffron, and the herbs. Warm over medium heat until broth is hot but not simmering.

Peel shrimp and carefully clean clams or mussels, discarding any that are not closed tightly. Scrub away sand and "beards." Add clams or mussels first and bring the bouillabaisse to a boil, watching carefully, for about 5 minutes, until they pop open. Discard any bivalves that do not open. Turn the heat down to low, add the mixed seafood and cook for another 5 minutes. Turn off the heat.

Serve with large chunks of fresh baked bread and sage butter.

Wine suggestion:

The light flavors of broth and seafood go well with viognier and chardonnay, but saffron gives this dish a dark yellow color and exotic aroma that also go well with pinot noir and sangiovese.

Halibut with Citrus Marinade

Halibut is sweet, tender and delicious—it cooks up fast, so all it needs is a quick citrus marinade and some fluffy rice.

2 8 oz. halibut filets
1 cup orange juice
Squeeze of lemon
1 tablespoon brown sugar or maple syrup
1 tablespoon fresh grated ginger root (about 2" of root, peeled)
1 teaspoon freshly crushed cardamom seeds (about eight pods), optional

Serves 2

In an 8" square glass pan, combine the orange juice, lemon, brown sugar, ginger root, and cardamom. Stir or whisk thoroughly. Pour half the mixture into a small saucepot and simmer over medium heat until the mixture reduces by a third to a half, and remove from heat. Place the halibut filets in the other half of the marinade for 15 minutes to two hours.

Broil the filets in the pan with their marinade, about 12" from the broiler, for two to three minutes on each side. Remove from heat and cover with a layer of aluminum foil and a kitchen towel for a few minutes. The halibut will continue to cook in its retained heat, while absorbing moisture from the marinade.

Serve with herbed rice or steamed vegetables, and a drizzle of the reduced marinade.

Wine suggestion:

Viognier, sauvignon blanc or a crisp, fruity chenin blanc.

Grilled Halibut with a Trinidad Glaze

"Put 'de lime in 'de coconut and grill 'de halibut." Try this dish in mid-winter for a hearty, tropical pick-me-up.

2 8 oz. halibut steaks
1 cup of coconut milk from 2 fresh soft-shelled coconuts[1] (or use canned coconut milk)
1 lime
1/2 teaspoon fresh lemon peel, grated, or dried lemon peel from Penzey's Spices
1 teaspoon Trinidad seasoning from Penzey's Spices
1 pod of cardamom seeds, crushed, optional
Sea salt to taste
2 tablespoons butter or margarine

Serves 2

Combine the coconut milk, lime juice, and seasonings in a small bowl. Whisk thoroughly.

In a sealable bag, marinate the halibut steaks with half of the coconut-lime mixture for at about 1/2 hour.

---

1.   Open each coconut by drilling or breaking two holes through the shell. Look for coconuts that have been pre-drilled so they will be easy to open. Place muslin or other coarse cloth over a small bowl, to catch any loose coconut fibers. Drain the coconut milk, which will be a watery, pale white color, into a small mixing bowl. Smell the coconut to check its quality. It should smell sweet and alluring. Save the coconut meat in the refrigerator—it can be scraped out and grated in a food processor, then frozen.

In a small saucepot, cook the remaining half of the marinade over low heat, simmering until reduced by a third, about 10 minutes. Add the butter one teaspoon at a time, stirring constantly, until the glaze begins to thicken and turn glossy. Remove from heat and allow to cool slightly. You should have about ¼ cup of glaze.

Grill the steaks over medium heat for 10 minutes, turning once after 5 minutes with a wide stainless steel spatula. Remove from heat and allow to rest for another 5-10 minutes. (Alternatively, you can broil the halibut for approximately the same amount of time.)

To serve, place each steak on a plate, and brush liberally with glaze. Serve with Peach-Ginger Salsa and a green salad.

Wine suggestion:

A crisp, delicate white like sauvignon blanc or a chilled, tropical powerhouse like viognier.

Manni's Seafood Pasta

Jan Manni of Atascadero, California gave us this recipe. Jan's daughter, Tessa, is one of friendly, knowledgeable staff you've encountered in our tasting room. This is the recipe that fuels Tessa's brilliant smile.

1 pound linguine
1 pound halibut, cut in 1" cubes
1 pound scallops
1 pound large prawns, deveined
1 yellow pepper, diced
1 red pepper, diced
3 tablespoons olive oil
2 tablespoons fresh garlic, finely chopped
1 white onion, peeled and finely chopped
4 firm, homegrown beefsteak or heirloom tomatoes, chopped into 1" pieces
2 oz. hard Parmesan, Reggiano or Asiago cheese
Fresh or dried oregano leaves

Serves 4-6

In a large skillet, sauté garlic, peppers, and onions in olive oil until tender and aromatic. Add the halibut, scallops, and prawns. Sauté briefly, no more than five minutes.
Cook the linguine in boiling, salted water until al dente, and drain.

Add chopped tomatoes to the seafood-vegetable mixture in the skillet and toss until the tomatoes are hot through.

Arrange the linguine in pasta bowls, and serve the seafood sauté over the linguine.

Grate fresh, hard cheese over each bowl, and garnish with fresh oregano leaves, or dried oregano, crushed with your fingertips. Serve with crusty Italian sourdough bread for sopping up the delicious leftover juices.

Wine suggestion:

Jan suggests a fruit-centered chardonnay.

Shrimp Caliente

Grilled tiger shrimp in a hot pants marinade.

2 pounds large tiger shrimp or prawns, peeled or butterflied[1]
1/4 cup white wine
2 tablespoons olive oil
3 garlic cloves, peeled and pressed
3 tablespoons fresh ginger root, peeled and grated
1 teaspoon Thai Fire Oil or chili oil
1/2 teaspoon red pepper flakes

Serves 6

Combine the wine, olive oil, garlic, ginger, chili oil, and red pepper. Whisk thoroughly. Place the prawns and marinade in a resealable bag or 8" glass pan and marinate for at least half an hour.

Grill the shrimp over medium hot coals for 3-5 minutes, turning occasionally. Remove when the shrimp are still pink but beginning to feel firm.

Wine suggestion:

A chilled viognier, a sangiovese, or a hearty zinfandel.

---

1.   To butterfly shrimp, use a pair of kitchen shears or a small knife to cut the shell from head to tail. Your guests can then easily peel the shells off as they dine. Leaving the shells on while grilling helps protect the shrimp from cooking too quickly, and creates little pockets for the marinade.

Shrimp and Asparagus Risotto

Risotto is easy, filling, and romantic. If you can make a good risotto, you will find your soulmate.

6 tablespoons olive oil
1 cup arborio rice
1 white onion, peeled and diced
1 cup mirapoix, optional (diced white onion, carrots, and celery)
2-3 cloves garlic, peeled, and diced or pressed
3-4 cups chicken broth
1 pound large shrimp or prawns, peeled
1/2 cup diced fresh poblano chile (or other mild chile)
1 cup fresh asparagus tips
1/2 cup grated Parmesan cheese

Serves 2

In a large skillet, warm the olive oil over medium heat. Add the rice and simmer for at least one minute, until the rice is translucent, a little longer for a toasted flavor and color.

Add the onion and simmer slowly until translucent and beginning to caramelize. Add the mirapoix and garlic, sauté until soft and fragrant.

Add a little chicken broth—just enough to completely cover the rice. Stir, and allow to simmer until almost all the liquid is absorbed. Continue to add broth in increments of about a cup until the rice is cooked through but still a little firm. (Taste tests are imperative.) Add the shrimp, diced chile and asparagus to the finished rice and cook just long enough for the shrimp and asparagus to turn bright, and for the shrimp to feel firm.

Add the cheese and stir quickly, just until it melts. Serve immediately.

Wine suggestion:

A rich chardonnay, spicy sangiovese, or old vine zinfandel.

Prawns in Ginger Peanut Sauce

Sticky peanut and ginger flavored prawns grilled on the barbecue make a great summer finger food.

2 pounds large tiger shrimp or prawns, peeled or butterflied
1/2 cup peanut butter
2 tablespoons maple syrup
2 tablespoons white Worcestershire sauce
1 teaspoon red pepper flakes
1 teaspoon Mongolian Fire Oil or chili oil
1/2 cup fresh squeezed orange juice
3-4" fresh ginger root, peeled and grated
Sea salt to taste

Serves 4

Combine all ingredients except the prawns in a medium glass bowl or 8" glass pan, and whisk thoroughly. If ingredients are cold and stiff, warm gently on the stove or grill, then mix. Set half the mixture aside to use as a dipping sauce.

Marinate the prawns in the remaining mixture for about half an hour.

Grill the prawns over medium hot coals for 3-5 minutes, turning once, and basting with any leftover marinade. Remove while still bright pink.

Serve with reserved dipping sauce, and Seattle Salad with Raspberry-Sesame Vinaigrette.

Wine suggestion:

A chilled viognier or sauvignon blanc, or a spicy sangiovese.

Salmon-stuffed Roasted Poblano Chiles

A touch of blue cheese and jalapeno in an easy blender-made stuffing, ready for grilling.

Roquefort and Gorgonzola cheeses are just two of the many blue-veined cheeses produced in the world, and the most common in American markets. Made in France under time-honored conditions that encourage indigenous yeasts, these cheeses feature blue veins running through the cheese, and a strong, aromatic character.

3 poblano chiles, halved and seeds removed
1 jalapeno
1 red bell pepper
1 tablespoon olive oil
6 oz. smoked salmon or lox (you can substitute crab if you prefer)
1/4 cup sour cream
2 oz. blue cheese
2 tablespoons fresh garlic chives, chopped
2 green onions, chopped
1/4 cup pine nuts, optional
4 oz. Colby or Gruyere cheese

Serves 6

Slice the jalapeno and red bell pepper in half, and remove the seeds. Rub lightly with olive oil and broil for 15 minutes, turning once, until peppers become tender. Allow to cool.

In a blender or food processor, blend the salmon, sour cream, and blue cheese. Finely dice the jalapenos and red bell pepper and gently stir into the mixture, reserving some of the bell pepper for garnish. Add the chopped green onions and pine nuts. Stuff each poblano half with the salmon mixture and grill over medium coals for 10 minutes, until the skins are soft and begin to turn brown. Cut the Colby or Gruyere into slices and put one slice over each pepper. Sprinkle with diced red pepper. Move the peppers to the exterior or low heat portion of the grill, cover and heat for 10 more minutes, until the cheese is melted and beginning to bubble. Serve immediately.

Wine suggestion:

Sangiovese or zinfandel.

Herb-Smoked Oysters with Grilled Sweet Pepper Salsa

Easy and entertaining—the smoky pepper salsa goes well with the earthy flavors of the oysters.

12 fresh oysters in the shell (buy extra in case some don't open)

Equipment needed:

Grill basket
Large tongs
Potholders
Stiff brush

For smoking:

3-4 large bunches of herbs ~ lavender, sage, rosemary, or thyme

Salsa:

2 cloves garlic, peeled and pressed, for basting
1/4 cup olive oil
1 red bell pepper, halved and seeds removed
1 yellow bell pepper, halved and seeds removed
1 orange bell pepper, halved and seeds removed
1 poblano chile
8 cloves garlic, peeled, for roasting
1 tablespoon red wine vinegar

Garnishes:

1 small bunch of fresh sage leaves
1 lemon, cut into 12 wedges

Serves 4

For smoking, place the herbs in a bucket of water to soak for at least an hour. Scrub the oysters well, cleaning off sand and algae. Discard any oysters that are not tightly closed or that do not close after handling.

In a small bowl, combine the pressed garlic and olive oil. Allow to steep for a few minutes while firing up the grill. Brush the bell peppers and poblano with some of the garlic-infused olive oil and grill over medium heat until the peppers begin to turn brown and become soft. Grill the garlic in a grill basket until soft and beginning to brown. Remove the peppers and garlic. When cool enough to handle, combine the peppers, poblano chile, garlic, remaining olive oil and vinegar in a food processor or blender and chop coarsely.

Add fresh coals and wait until the temperature at grill level is so hot that you can't hold your hand 3 inches away. Set oysters around the outside of the grill, with the flat side of the shell down, and the cupped side up. As the oysters open, the seawater inside will flush out onto the coals, so have extra coals handy and some way to add them as you're grilling. As the oysters open, remove them from the grill, using a potholder to handle them. Open them completely and slide a small knife under the muscle to cut it.

At this stage, the oysters are hot through, but still somewhat raw. Serve them up fresh with a tiny dollop of grilled salsa, a slice of lemon, and a sage leaf.

For those who like their oysters fully cooked, put enough wet herbs on the coals to diffuse the heat and create some aromatic smoke—about one handful. Lightly oil a grill basket and place the oysters inside with space between each. Set the grill basket on the grill and close the barbecue lid for two minutes. Remove the grill basket and serve the oysters immediately.

To serve, tuck a lemon wedge and sage leaf against the back slope of a clean shell. Hold in place and ladle a spoonful of the grilled pepper mixture into the shell. Lay a smoked oyster on top and serve.

Wine suggestion:

Chardonnay, sangiovese, pinot noir, or zinfandel.

Tako Poke Salad

Tako Poke is one of our favorite Hawaiian delicacies. We've given it an international spin with chiles, Armenian cucumbers, balsamic vinegar and Romaine lettuce.
Tako (tah-koe) is the Japanese word for octopus, and poke (poh-kee) is a Hawaiian dish of raw, cubed fish, found all over the islands in hundreds of versions. Tako poke is one of our favorites, but it's generally made with a super-hot Korean kimchee sauce. This is a tamer version that will go well with wine.

1 pound fresh, cleaned, tenderized baby octopus
(Large 1 to 2 pound octopii are better for slow cooking—you'll want small legs and bodies for this salad. If your local fish market doesn't carry them separately, they may have a "seafood medley" you can buy—pick out the octopus meat and freeze the rest for a pasta dish later.)
1/4 cup sesame oil (good quality toasted sesame oil is a dark brown color)
2 teaspoons tamari (high-quality soy sauce)
2 teaspoons balsamic vinegar
1 teaspoon white wine vinegar
1 bunch green onions, finely chopped
1 Armenian or English cucumber, peeled and finely diced
1 Hungarian hot wax pepper, seeds removed and finely diced
1 head Romaine lettuce
1 beefsteak or heirloom tomato
1 tablespoon toasted sesame seeds

Serves 4

On the mainland, octopus is generally only available frozen or previously frozen, which is desirable, since freezing tenderizes the meat. Ask for cleaned octopus, with ink sacs, organs and beaks removed. At good fish markets, you can get octopus already cleaned, tenderized and cut into pieces. They may even parboil it for you on request.

Thaw the octopus in cold water, drain and pat dry, then cut into bite size pieces. Cook in boiling water for 3-5 minutes, until the meat is firm but still squeaky. Drain and cool in the refrigerator or freezer.

Combine the octopus, sesame oil, tamari, vinegars, onions, cucumber, and diced pepper. Marinating improves the flavor, but it can be served immediately.

Tear the Romaine leaves into bite-size pieces and make a fluffy pile on each plate. Cut the tomato into wedges and arrange 2-3 slices over the Romaine. Top with a large spoonful of tako poke, and sprinkle with toasted sesame seeds.

Wine suggestion:

Our favorite pairing was a Cloudy Bay sauvignon blanc from New Zealand, but a crisp malvasia bianca or chenin blanc would also be wonderful.

On the Grill

Ten Easy Grilling Tips

It all boils down to *how do I get it started?* and *when is it done?* Everything in between should be simple and fun. Dan and I grill appetizers for hundreds of people on wine festival weekends. For the most part, we've had great success, except when I set fire to the barbecue itself (a feat Dan didn't think possible), or the time our friends decided to use walnut firewood to start a twelve-hour barbecue fire, good for dinner *and* breakfast. While this might not inspire a lot of trust in my grilling advice, please let me point out that we have learned a lot from our grilling adventures.

We use a Weber kettle-style barbecue, because we like the intense heat produced by coals, as well as even heating when the lid is closed. Our 26" Weber can get up to 600° very quickly with the lid closed. We don't actually grill at that temperature, in our saner moments, but we can grill on cold, windy evenings while we're working on the crush pad, without losing heat to wind and frigid outdoor temperatures. We also have a gas grill, which is a great backup for busy grill evenings, but we've found that in cold, windy conditions gas flames just cannot keep the grill hot enough, even with the lid closed. Gas emitters clog with grease and ash, and since we grill often, that's extremely inconvenient. So we stick with our trusty Weber, piling coals in the middle for a nice hot center, and leaving the edges open for radiant heat, or piling them to one side if we're going to rotisserie. We can also use moistened wood chips and herbs in a coal barbecue.

Here are our ten simple steps for successful and enjoyable grilling:

Give yourself plenty of time.

Time to get the coals started, time to prepare and marinate the meat, time to cook the meat slowly over medium-hot coals. Grilling is not an activity that should be rushed. Give yourself an early start so you can visit with guests and enjoy a leisurely pace.

Set up a comfortable work area

Grilling is fun, and it should be relaxing, so there's something to be said for starting the evening with dry coals, a clean grill, a grill brush that still has plenty of wires on it, and a lighter that works. We purchased a Rubbermaid storage unit to hold all our grilling detritus like extra coals, paper grocery bags, old pots, drip pans, mesquite chips, wooden skewers and toothpicks for serving sausage. It keeps everything dry and out of sight, and gives us extra counter space next to the barbecue.

Make sure you've got space nearby for a cutting board, spices, a knife, and barbecue tools.

Use a starter chimney

We suggest using a grill chimney to start the coals. Lighter fluid and self-lighting coals impart a chemical flavor and aroma to grilled foods. Plus, they're generally more expensive. With practice, a chimney makes starting coals easier (and in some cases safer) than any other method.

Paper mashing is an art. Don't mash too much paper into the bottom of the chimney or air won't be able to feed the flames. If the chimney paper and coals don't cheerfully ignite, just tip the chimney at an angle for a minute to allow air to flow under the flames and paper.

Keep the grill clean

At Dover Canyon, keeping the grill clean is a matter of debate. Dan prefers plenty of "char" on the grill, making it less likely that food will stick. Mary says congealed, half-life grease looks nasty when black bits of it show up on seafood. Therefore, we keep an old grill and a new one on hand, so there's always a clean grill, or one that's relatively easy to brush clean, for fish, shellfish, and lighter meats.

To remove excess char, get the grill hot over the coals, then brush vigorously with a stiff wire brush. A painter's wire brush will work better and last longer than the fussy versions sold as barbecue accessories.

Go for the allover sear

To keep red meats tender and juicy, it's very important to turn your meat frequently, over fairly hot coals, for the first few minutes. Even a slight sear will help to seal in moisture. Light meats and fish do not need a charred exterior, just a quick sizzle on each side. Thicker cuts of meat benefit from being turned frequently at first while the coals are still hot so they get that yummy, crusty exterior with the pretty char marks. Marinades and bastes are very important for this step—a little extra sugar in the marinade will help it adhere, and the meat will caramelize quickly, sealing in moisture, juice, and heat. Tilt cuts of meat on their edges briefly to seal all sides of the cut.

There are two camps on basting philosophy—one camp claims that basting prevents crispy caramelization, and the other camp claims that basting keeps grilled cuts moist. Our findings, after hundreds of field trials, are that red meats should be allowed to caramelize over high heat, then moved to the edge of the grill to continue roasting. Fish, on the other hand, should be grilled over lower heat, with frequent basting to keep the fish moist and succulent. We encourage you to perform your own field trials.

Don't overcook

Always err on the moist, underdone side. Grill temperatures can be quite hot, and after food is removed from the grill, it will continue to cook in its own retained heat. You can always return meat to the grill, so if you think it's almost done, place the meat on a cutting board and let it rest for several minutes. Cutting a thin slice off the end will give you a good idea of how the center is doing.

While turning meat to caramelize the exterior, remember that barbecue sauces have quite an impact at this stage. The more sugar in the sauce, the faster the exterior will seal. Move large cuts of meat slightly off center to continue cooking near, but not directly over, the hottest coals, or all the way out to the edge to heat all the way through without boiling out the meat juices.

After searing, grill your meat on each side of the cut for two to ten minutes at a time, depending on the thickness of the cut. A T-bone steak one to two inches thick would need to cook an additional four to five minutes on each side, while a triangular tritip cut would need about ten minutes on each side.

Feeling for doneness—the "jelly test"

Grilling is not always done in early evening, with warm breezes wafting through a chartreuse canopy of spring walnut leaves. We enjoy those evenings, but we've also been known to grill a roast in the kitchen window's castoff light on a cold, crisp November night while waiting for a star shower.

We recommend the use of a good meat thermometer, but if you don't have one (or can't find it), another way to test grilled meat for doneness is to give it the "jelly" test. If it feels wiggly when you squeeze it with tongs, it's a long way from done. When meat starts to firm up, it's hot and probably cooked through.

Remove the meat to the radiant heat portion of the grill and check the interior by slicing it slightly open with a knife.

Remember the radiant

When meat is removed from the grill, it will continue to develop toward doneness, just as a roast would, from its own retained heat. Keeping this in mind is doubly important if you use a sweet marinade to sear the meat. Your grill meat will have an "envelope" that not only holds in juice, but heat as well.

To ensure the center of a large cut is done, cover the meat with two layers of aluminum foil and a kitchen towel for 10-15 minutes. If the meat is done on the outside, but you would like the interior to cook a little more, this technique allows the center to heat through without applying more char to the exterior.

Keep a bag of mesquite chips on hand

Soak mesquite chips in water, so you don't set the barbecue on fire. If your coals have died down, a single dry wood chip or two will help flame up new coals without the chemical off-gassing of lighter fluid, but don't—trust me, don't—add more than one or two.

Wet mesquite added to coals will create soft, smoky flavors during radiant heat cooking. Since you only need to use a few chips at a time, one small bag should last through several grilling sessions.

Soak herb wood for laying on the coals

If you have an herb garden, this is a great way to use deadwood from perennial herbs that need to be pruned back. Harvest an armful of overgrown wood, soak them in a bucket of water for an hour, and apply a handful at a time to very hot coals. We usually perform this step after caramelizing the exterior of large cuts, and right before we close the lid.

Tarragon stems contribute a heady licorice scent which is nice with fatty red meats. Lavender has a floral, slightly bitter and pungent aroma, terrific with lamb. Oregano gives off a spicy, Italian scent, and rosemary creates a romantic, mouth-watering incense.

Grilled Portabellas with Gorgonzola

Easy to make, yet hearty and satisfying, great with a robust red wine like syrah.

6 to 12 medium-size portabella mushrooms, about 4" across
1/4 cup olive oil
1 tablespoon balsamic vinegar
6 oz. Gorgonzola cheese
Mild, colorful peppers, seeds removed and diced (optional)

Serves 6, or 2 winemakers

Combine the olive oil and balsamic vinegar in a small bowl and whisk. Baste the mushrooms lightly with the olive oil mixture. Sprinkle a spoonful of Gorgonzola over each mushroom and top with diced peppers. Grill over medium coals with the lid partially closed, until the cheese is melted and the mushrooms are soft but still firm enough to lift. Carefully lift from the grill with a wide metal spatula and allow to cool slightly before serving.

Serve as an hors d'oeuvre, or a side dish with grilled meats.

Wine suggestion:

Pinot noir, sangiovese, cabernet, or syrah.

Grilled Chile and Cheese Sandwiches

Roasted chiles and caramelized onions give this version of our beloved toasted cheese sandwich a decidedly adult twist.

1 loaf shepherd's bread, ½" thick slices
8 tablespoons olive oil
2 white or sweet onions
1 red bell pepper
1 yellow bell pepper
1 poblano pepper
1 anaheim pepper
1/2 pound Longhorn cheddar or Monterey Jack cheese, grated

Serves 4

Peel the onions and cut into thin slices. Warm 6 tablespoons olive oil in a large frypan, and caramelize the onions over medium heat for about 20 minutes, until brown and sweet. Turn off the heat and set aside.

Halve the peppers and remove the seeds. Cut each half into 1" wide strips. Grill the pepper segments in a grill basket over medium-hot coals, basting with remaining olive oil, until soft, aromatic, and beginning to char. Remove to the radiant heat portion of the grill, and toast the bread over medium coals until lightly browned on both sides.

Assemble the sandwiches by stacking one slice of bread, ¼ of the cheese, mixed slices of pepper, ¼ of the caramelized onions, and another slice of bread. Lightly baste the outside of each sandwich with olive oil. Place on the grill over low coals, close the lid, and heat for 1-2 minutes, until the cheese is melted and just beginning to drip.

Slice the sandwiches into small wedges to serve as hors d'oeuvres, or for dipping into chili, soups, or bouillabaisse. Or just carve them in half for hungry crush crews.

Wine suggestion:

A cold brew or a spicy zinfandel.

The Renegade Burger

Nothing is simpler than a good ol' burger with vegies and condiments piled on top. With these delicious toppings, you'll need a couple of pine boards on hand just to squeeze them down to chewing size.

2 pounds lean ground round
1/4 cup toasted bread crumbs
1 egg, optional
3 tablespoons fresh thyme, chopped fine
Salt and pepper to taste
6-8 hamburger buns or French rolls

Grilled Toppings:

3 cloves garlic, peeled and crushed or diced
1/4 cup olive oil
2 large white onions or sweet Mayan onions, cut in ¼" slices
2 poblano peppers, seeds removed and sliced into 1" strips
2 beefsteak or heirloom tomatoes, cut into ½" slices

Fresh Toppings:

2 cups mixed mesclun greens
1 cup fresh arugula
2 avocados, pitted and sliced (buy an extra avocado if you're unsure about quality)

Serves 6

Whisk the egg, then add the ground round, crumbs, thyme and seasonings. Combine thoroughly with your hands and form into 1" thick patties about 4" across. Put the garlic in the olive oil and allow to infuse for 15 minutes or longer, while the coals get hot.

Slather some garlic-infused olive oil over the onions, peppers, and tomatoes, and toast them on the grill, either directly or in a grill basket, until tender and lightly browned. Set aside on an attractive platter. Clean and prepare fresh toppings and serve in bowls.

Grill the patties over medium-hot coals, turning frequently. Grill the buns until toasty. Serve the patties and buns immediately. Let your guests build their own burger with Chipotle Mayo, Sundried Tomato Catsup and Viognier-French Tarragon Mustard.

Wine suggestion:

We named this burger for our delicious table wine, Renegade Red.

CHIPOTLE MAYO

Chipotles are smoked jalapenos—very, very hot! They come folded up and preserved in their own sauce in 3 to 7 oz. cans.

2 cups mayonnaise
2 teaspoons chipotle sauce

Stir two teaspoons of chipotle sauce into the mayonnaise, and reserve the rest of the chipotles in a jar or plastic container for winter chilis and BBQ sauces.

Makes 2 cups

SUNDRIED TOMATO CATSUP

Sundried tomatoes give this homemade catsup an exotic smoky flavor that's great with burgers and roast beef sandwiches.

1 29 oz. can tomato sauce
3 tablespoons brown sugar or molasses
1/3 cup white wine
1/3 cup chopped, sundried tomatoes in oil

2 tablespoons oil from sundried tomatoes
4-5 cloves garlic, peeled, roasted and mashed
1 tablespoon fresh grated ginger root
1/4 teaspoon sea salt
1/4 teaspoon freshly ground black peppercorn

Makes about 1 ½ cups

Roast or sauté the garlic, then mash. Roasted garlic tastes best, but if you're in a hurry, just sauté it for 5 minutes in one teaspoon olive oil until soft and aromatic. Combine all ingredients and bring to a boil over medium heat. Immediately lower the heat so that the sauce barely bubbles, and simmer for 1-2 hours, until reduced by about one-third. Allow to cool. Store in a clean jar or plastic container. Keeps for about two weeks, refrigerated.

Viognier-French Tarragon Mustard

Fresh and spicy, with an intriguing hint of licorice

1/2 cup brown mustard seed (available from Penzey's Spices)
1/4 cup viognier
1/4 cup chicken broth
1 tablespoon brown sugar
4 sprigs fresh tarragon, destemmed and finely chopped
1/4 teaspoon fresh cardamom seed, crushed (optional)

Makes about 1 cup

Place the mustard seed, white wine, and chicken broth in a glass bowl, stir until the seeds sink, and refrigerate overnight. The following day crush the mustard seed in a food processor or coffee grinder until well-broken, to a rough mustard consistency. Pulse and then pat down with a spoon, pulse and repeat. The seeds tend to fly around and are too small for most electric processors, so the mustard will still have lots of whole seeds. Add the brown sugar, tarragon, and cardamom seed, and pulse some more. The final mustard will be super-strong and very crunchy. Store in a clean glass jar or plastic container. Keeps for 2 weeks, refrigerated. Use sparingly on sandwiches or as a condiment for meats.

New Zealand Baby Rack of Lamb

Simply prepared grilled lamb ribs, juicy, mouth-watering and pink.

We grill lamb racks all day on wine festival weekends. We offer a small bowl of the lavender-flecked herb rub so visitors can grab a pinch to taste, or sprinkle a little more over their lamb. The salty rub gives the bite-size ribs a nice, crusty exterior—a perfect complement to the pink, juicy meat within.

2 racks of baby New Zealand lamb
1/2 teaspoon sea salt
1 tablespoon herbs de Provence (or a blend of dried sage, thyme and lavender blossoms)
1 tablespoon freshly cracked black peppercorn
Additional stems of lavender, optional
Rosemary branches, optional

Serves 4

Mix the sea salt, herbs and ground pepper together. Rub each rack with some of the herb and salt mixture.

Over hot coals, sear the exterior of the racks on both sides and on the thick edge, being careful not to burn the exposed bones. Move the racks to the exterior portion of the grill for about 10 minutes. Lay the bones over the edge of the grill so they don't burn. When done, each individual rib should be uniformly cooked, with a firm texture, but still juicy in the interior.

Serve with Cranberry-Tequila Salsa and Gorgonzola Mashed Potatoes.

Wine suggestion:

A rich red wine with medium to heavy tannins—zinfandel, cabernet sauvignon, or syrah.

Cranberry-Tequila Salsa

1/4 cup Tequila
2 yellow Hungarian wax peppers, seeds removed, diced
1/3 fresh ginger root, peeled and grated
2 cloves garlic, peeled and mashed with a garlic press
2 12 oz. cans whole cranberry sauce
6 green onions, chopped
1/2 bunch fresh cilantro, chopped

Serves 6-8

Combine the Tequila, diced Hungarian wax peppers, grated ginger root and garlic in a small bowl. Allow the mixture to rest for 5 minutes or more. The Tequila will extract flavor from the other ingredients. Combine the cranberry sauce, onions and cilantro, then stir in the Tequila mixture. Serve as a condiment with red meats.

Garlic and Herb London Broil

This recipe was contributed by Bruce and Sandy Shomler, owners of Sycamore Farms in Paso Robles, California. Visitors to their herb farm leave with armfuls of potted herbs, cut lemon grass, and quart bags of basil, thyme, chives, and arugula. Gourmet cooks and avid wine collectors, Bruce and Sandy are also part owners of Chequera Vineyard, a lovely terraced slope of syrah and viognier surrounding the herb farm.

2 pounds London broil
1/4 cup olive oil
1/4 cup apple cider vinegar
1 cup combined fresh chopped thyme, rosemary and sage
4 cloves garlic, peeled and chopped
1 tablespoon sea salt
1/3 cup Worcestershire sauce

Serves 6

To make the marinade, combine the olive oil, apple cider vinegar, herbs, garlic, salt and Worcestershire and mix well.

Place the meat in a large plastic bag or large bowl. Pour the marinade over and seal. Marinate in the refrigerator for at least 24 hours, turning several times to make sure the marinade touches all sides of the meat. Remove meat, and pour the marinade into a bowl for basting the meat when grilling.

Grill over hot coals for about 5 minutes on each side. Transfer the meat to a cutting board and let stand for about 5 minutes. Carve into 1/4 inch slices and serve immediately.

Wine suggestion:

A spicy red like sangiovese or zinfandel pairs well with the fresh herbs, but traditional choices like syrah, merlot, or cabernet sauvignon are also delicious.

Rib Eye Steak with Caramelized Onions and Mushrooms

This hearty dish is a classic, simple way to prepare a hearty meal. Start the coals, leave the onions and mushrooms to slowly caramelize, take a shower, pour a glass of wine, and throw the steaks on ready coals. Perfect for Monday night football.

2 large rib eye steaks, prime or choice
4 cloves garlic, slivered
Sage salt rub (1 tablespoon each dried, crumbled sage, sea salt, and freshly ground black pepper)
1 large white onion, thinly sliced
1/4 cup olive oil
1/4 cup butter
30 Italian brown mushrooms, sliced

Serves 4 normal people or 2 winemakers

Cut small slits in the steaks, and insert slivers of garlic deep into the steaks. Rub the steaks on both sides with the sage rub and set them aside.

In a large frypan, warm the olive oil, one tablespoon of butter, and add the sliced white onion. Sauté over medium-low heat for about 10 minutes, then add the mushrooms and continue to sauté until the onions are well caramelized and the mushrooms are dark and soft, another 20 minutes. The mushrooms will initially absorb the oil and butter, but as they soften they will release the oil and some moisture, so just be patient—have a glass of wine.

Grill the steaks over hot coals, turning quickly to sear on both sides, and then move the steaks to the outer portion of the grill to heat through, about 10 minutes on both sides. Remove from the grill and let the steaks rest for 5-10 minutes before serving. Top with a generous portion of caramelized onions and mushrooms. Serve with mashed or grilled potatoes.

Wine suggestion:

Serve with a cabernet sauvignon, Bordeaux-style blend, or a robust syrah.

Colin's Pepper Plant Porterhouse

My son Colin loves Pepper Plant seasoning. It goes on his potatoes, meats, eggs, even potato chips. This is his version of grilled porterhouse steaks—and it was a hit with Dan, as well.

2 large porterhouse steaks, prime or choice
10 cloves garlic, peeled and sliced
1/2 bottle of barbecue sauce, your choice
1/2 glass of red wine
2 shots of Tequila
Several squirts each of white and dark Worcestershire sauce
3 tablespoons Pepper Plant seasoning sauce
2 tablespoons A-1 steak sauce
2 dashes Tabasco
Dash of dried dill weed
Sea salt and fresh ground black pepper, to taste

Serves 2 hungry people

Cut small slits in the Porterhouse, and insert slivers of garlic deep into the steaks. Combine all the marinade ingredients in a glass pan or resealable bag and marinate the steaks overnight, or for at least two hours.

Sprinkle with salt and pepper just before grilling. Grill the steaks over hot coals, turning quickly to sear on both sides, and then move the steaks to the outer portion of the grill to heat through, about 5 minutes on each side. Remove from the grill and let the steaks rest for 5-10 minutes before serving. Serve with Triple Threat Mashed Potatoes.

Wine suggestion:

Serve with a cabernet, or a robust syrah.

Grilled Tritip in a Beer and Chipotle Marinade

Smoky chipotles and a little molasses give the meat a rich, smoky flavor.
Tritip is a boneless beef roast cut from the bottom sirloin. It is also called "triangular roast" because of its shape. Tritips vary from 1½ to 3 pounds, and are about 2 inches thick. When cooked to rare in the center, the thinner outside edges are medium to well done, offering perfectly prepared beef for every taste.

1 2-3 pound tritip
3 garlic cloves, peeled and slivered
Sea salt and fresh ground black pepper
1 1/2 cups beer (chef's choice)
1 chipotle, chopped
1/4 cup molasses
Fresh rosemary and sage leaves, about 1 handful, stripped and chopped

Serves 6

Cut 1/2" deep slits into the tritip and insert slivers of garlic. Massage the exterior of the tritip with sea salt and black pepper. Thoroughly mix the beer, chipotle, and molasses. Strip rosemary leaves off the stems and add the rosemary and chopped sage to the marinade. Marinate the meat for 1-2 hours. Grill over hot coals for 10 minutes, turning frequently to caramelize the exterior, then cook over radiant heat for another 20-30 minutes, depending on the size of the cut. Use the "jelly test" or cut off an end piece to check for doneness.

Serve with Gorgonzola Potatoes and a green salad.

Wine suggestion:

A really big zinfandel or syrah.

Grilled Tritip in a Late Harvest Zinfandel and Black Pepper Marinade

Tritip in a sweet, thick marinade with tons of freshly cracked black pepper.

1 2-3 pound untrimmed Black Angus tritip
2 tablespoons sea salt
3 cloves garlic, peeled and slivered
1 cup late harvest zinfandel (or raspberry jam)
1 handful fresh tarragon leaves, stripped from stems and coarsely chopped
1 handful fresh rosemary leaves, stripped from stems
1/4 cup coarsely ground black peppercorn
   (Freshly ground pepper gives this dish the most exciting flavor—an electric coffee grinder will make fast work of grinding peppercorns.)
Rosemary, sage, or thyme branches, optional

Serves 6-8

Trim the fat off the bottom and edge of the tritip. Rub one tablespoon of sea salt all over the tritip. Using a small, sharp knife, cut ½" slits in the tritip and insert a sliver of garlic in each slit. In a small bowl combine the late harvest wine or jam, tarragon, rosemary, most of the ground pepper and remaining salt. Save the rest of the pepper for sprinkling over the tritip while it's grilling. Marinate the tritip in a resealable gallon bag for at least ½ hour.

Place the tritip on the grill and save the zinfandel-pepper marinade for basting. Grill the tritip directly over high heat for 10 minutes, turning often. The sweet marinade will caramelize the meat's exterior, sealing in juices and helping the pepper to adhere. Baste occasionally with the remaining marinade, and sprinkle with more pepper. When the exterior is caramelized, move the tritip to the radiant heat portion of the grill and cook, covered, at 450° to 550° for 15-20 minutes, turning occasionally and basting with additional marinade and pepper.

You can put moistened rosemary directly on the coals at this stage for an herb-and-smoke flavor. We pick rosemary branches a few hours before grilling, and place them in a bucket of water, with a plate on top to hold them down. This is a good way to use prunings of old wood from rosemary, sage, and thyme. It gives grill smoke an incense-like aroma and imparts an interesting flavor to grilled meats. Plan to cook the meat for an additional 5-15 minutes due to reduced temperature.

When the meat is firm and appears to be done, remove and allow to rest for 5-10 minutes under two layers of aluminum foil and two dishtowels.

Garnish with additional sprigs of tarragon and serve with Gorgonzola Mashed Potatoes and a Mesclun Salad with Raspberries and Black Pepper.

Wine suggestion:

A deep, spicy zinfandel.

Tequila Chicken

Tequila, brown sugar, garlic, and garden chiles in a wonderfully sticky marinade.

8 chicken legs and thighs, bone-in
2 tablespoons Tequila
2 cloves garlic, peeled and pressed
1 red chile, seeds removed and diced (or 1/2 teaspoon red pepper flakes)
3 tablespoons brown sugar or molasses
1 lime
Salt and pepper
1/2 red bell pepper, seeds removed and finely diced
Fresh cilantro for garnish

Serves 4

Combine the Tequila, garlic, red chile, brown sugar and the juice of one lime in a small non-reactive bowl.

Clean the chicken pieces and pat dry. Rub with salt and pepper. Place the chicken and marinade in a non-reactive container or sealable bag and marinate for at least 1/2 hour to overnight.

Grill over medium-hot coals for 20-25 minutes, reserving marinade for basting. Turn and baste frequently. The marinade will pre-cook the chicken slightly, so watch closely while grilling and remove the chicken while still moist.

Garnish with fresh cilantro and diced red bell pepper. Serve with grilled potatoes and vegetables.

Wine suggestion:

Serve with chardonnay, zinfandel or sangiovese.

Chicken in Thai Fire Oil

A spicy, Asian style marinade on the exterior, juicy chicken inside.

4 boneless, skinless chicken breasts
Salt and pepper
1/4 cup honey
2 cloves garlic, peeled and pressed
3 tablespoons Thai fire oil or chili oil
2 tablespoons white Worcestershire sauce
1 sweet Meyer lemon

Serves 4

Clean the chicken breasts and pat dry. Rub with salt and pepper. Combine the other ingredients in a basting pan or small glass bowl and warm gently on the grill or in the microwave until the honey is warm. Stir or whisk thoroughly. Pour over the chicken and marinate for 15-45 minutes in an 8" glass pan or sealable bag.

Grill over medium-hot coals for 10-15 minutes, or broil in the center of the oven at 500° for 10-15 minutes on each side—until golden brown outside, but still juicy inside. Boneless breasts cook faster than chicken with the bone-in, so if you're not sure, err on the moist side. Remove the chicken when it begins to feel firm and allow it to sit for a few minutes, covered with foil. To test for doneness, use a sharp paring knife to separate the meat near the center of the breast. The meat should be creamy white and still exuding pink juice.

Serve with Seattle Salad, or with steamed asparagus and jasmine rice.

Wine suggestion:

The tropical flavors of a chilled viognier or Rhône white are perfect with the incendiary, exotic flavors in this marinade.

The Harvest Kitchen

Cooking with Wine

Cooking with wine is easier than most people realize. We use wine in basting sauces, marinades, vinaigrettes, and other dishes that customarily call for a dash of lemon or vinegar. It doesn't take a lot of wine to flavor a dish. Begin with a few tablespoons, let it simmer, and taste it again when the alcohol has evaporated. Like lemon juice, wine has a "cooking" effect of its own, so meat dishes might cook faster. Be watchful, taste as you go, and have fun.

Always use a good wine for cooking—alcohol evaporates during simmering, leaving only the flavor of wine in your sauce. Wines labeled "cooking wine," or old wines that have turned acetic will give disappointing results. Recipes seldom call for more than a cup of wine, so why not buy a premium wine and enjoy the same wine with your meal?

Love me tender...

Acids, alcohol, sugar, salt, and enzymes all have a tenderizing effect on meat. This doesn't sound very appetizing, initially, until you realize that many of our favorite barbecue sauces and marinade ingredients contribute tenderness as well as flavor. The acid family, for instance, includes balsamic and wine vinegars, citrus juices, and tomatoes. For alcohols, I prefer wine, wine, Tequila, and rum. Sugars include white and brown sugar, molasses, honey, and sweet fruits. For salt, you can use sea salt, soy sauce, or tamari. The enzyme family calls in pineapple, papaya, kiwi, and ginger.

Basically, tenderizing breaks long muscle tissue down into short, digestibly delicious muscle tissues. A thin calamari steak is effectively tenderized by beating it into a pancake, which can then be dipped in egg yolk and bread crumbs and sautéed into a light, fluffy calamari steak. Beating a ten pound tenderloin will not have much effect, however, so it's best to buy a high-quality meat with plenty of marbling, and plan to roast it slowly.

Everything in between—like chicken breasts and thighs, steaks, thick-cut pork chops, and ribs—will benefit from a little time in a tenderizing-slash-barbecue sauce.

It isn't necessary to overthink the sauce. For instance, if you have pork, any sweet fruit like apricots and papaya, combined with ginger and maybe molasses, are a sure-fire winner. Chicken handles anything from salt rubs through tomatoes to fruit-and-chile combinations. Let your taste buds guide you, and simply enjoy the knowledge that many of the ingredients you are adding for flavor will also help tenderize the meat.

If you're using a salt or herb rub, brush or massage the mixture vigorously into the meat for tenderizing.

Using wine in a tenderizing sauce is a traditional way to cook poultry and game. Various recipes for Coq au Vin suggest different ways of combining wine and herbs, and this traditional dish of wine, chicken, and herbs can be made with white or red wine, and either baked in the oven or simmered on the stove.

Reduction Sauces

The berry and plum flavors of merlot and zinfandel are well suited for reduction sauces, which are excellent with pork tenderloin, lamb, and other rich but tender meats. A reduction sauce is a simple confection of basically two ingredients—balsamic vinegar and butter. The idea is to simmer two cups of vinegar until it's reduced by a third to half its volume, and then slowly whisk in eight tablespoons of cold butter until the mixture becomes a silky, sensuous sauce.

The whole idea is greatly improved by substituting some wine for part of the vinegar, and tossing in a few herbs along the way.

To make a *beurre rouge* reduction sauce, combine one cup balsamic vinegar with one cup of red wine in a small saucepan, plus a few tablespoons of diced white onions and herbs if desired. Cook over medium heat until the volume is reduced by half. Strain the mixture and discard any solids.

Return the sauce to the pan, reduce heat to low, and add eight tablespoons (one stick) of butter, one tablespoon at a time, stirring constantly until the sauce is thick and glossy.

Sauces and Marinades

Dessert wines are excellent for marinades. Their combination of alcohol and sugar gently tenderizes while marinating, and you can follow up the meal with small glasses of the wine served with crispy cookies and nuts for an instant dessert.

Cornish game hens are delicious basted with a wine sauce of late harvest zinfandel combined with raspberries or cranberries—for a white wine version, combine a white dessert wine with dried apricots and golden raisins. Frozen fruit should be rinsed in a colander under hot water first, and dried fruit should be soaked in water or apple juice for at least an hour.

To grill, butterfly each hen by cutting upward along each side of the spine so the hen can be flattened, then baste thoroughly and rub the fruit well into the skin before grilling. Add fresh or dried fruit to wild rice, and serve with grilled or roasted root vegetables.

Vinaigrettes

Vinaigrettes and antipasto marinades are easy to make with wine, which is softer and less acidic than many vinegars. For a white wine vinaigrette, use a good quality olive oil, fine white wine, and fresh chopped herbs. Mix the ingredients in a bowl, adding a little at a time, and tasting as you go. I recommend starting with two parts olive oil and one part white wine. Transfer the vinaigrette to a serving bottle or jar when you are happy with the flavors and balance. I often make a salad dressing "on the fly" and use it moments later, but you can also make enough to fill a jar or bottle, and keep it in the refrigerator. Spice and herb flavors will marry with the oil and wine, and the vinaigrette will only improve.

For a red vinaigrette, use olive oil, red wine, herbs, and maybe a touch of aged balsamic vinegar for depth. Start with one part balsamic or red wine vinegar to four parts olive oil, and adjust to taste. Spices add interesting flavors, and by using them creatively, you can get gentler and more flavorful dressings than commercial varieties. Dill, oregano, thyme, and rosemary are always good in a vinaigrette—you can either shake in some ground, dried herbs or chop and add fresh herbs. Cardamom seed has an orange-like flavor that is nice with white wine. Try cloves, nutmeg, or freshly ground black peppercorn with red wine vinaigrettes or marinades.

If you're not sure about the flavor of wine in a particular dish, set a small amount of your ingredients aside, and mix in some wine and herbs. Taste and adjust before adding the wine to your creation. Have fun, be creative, and remember to pour a glass of wine for the cook.

Eggplant and Calamari Parmesan

Dan came up with this lovely, layered dish one night when he couldn't decide whether to Parmesan the eggplant or the calamari.

1 medium eggplant, sliced about 1/4" inch thick
2 calamari steaks
1/4 cup olive oil
2 cloves garlic, peeled and diced
2 egg yolks
1 cup dried bread crumbs
1 16 oz. jar marinara sauce
2 cups grated Parmesan cheese
2 cups Mozzarella cheese
Sea salt to taste

Serves 2

Layer the eggplant slices in a large colander and sprinkle them with salt. Let them rest for at least half an hour. In the meantime, pound out the calamari steaks. To pound out the steaks, place them, one at a time, on a large cutting board. Cover the steaks with plastic wrap (to prevent pieces of fish from flying all over the kitchen while you're pounding on it). Starting at the center of the steak and working out toward the edges, pound the calamari thoroughly with a meat tenderizer, rolling pin, or empty wine bottle. The calamari should be spread thin and translucent, but not torn.

In a 12" frypan, warm the olive and garlic. Whisk the egg yolks and pour onto a plate. Spread the bread crumbs on another plate. Dip the eggplant slices into the egg, then into the bread crumbs. Sauté each eggplant slice until translucent, and remove. Repeat with the calamari and sauté until firm.

Grease a 9" x 9" glass pan. Beginning with a slice of eggplant, layer eggplant, marinara, Parmesan and Mozzarella, then calamari, marinara and cheese until you have three or four layers, depending on the thickness of the eggplant slices. Finish with a layer of Parmesan.

Bake in a 400° oven for about 20 minutes—until the layers are set and the cheese is melted.

Serve with a green salad.

Wine suggestion:

Chardonnay, sangiovese or zinfandel.

Sweet Corn Seafood Chowder

Seafood lightly sautéed with jalapeno, added to black beans and corn in a Veracruz-style chowder.

If Mexico were a shrimp, you would find Veracruz tucked inside the curve of its tail. Poised along the Gulf of Mexico, its cuisine features snapper, oyster, shrimp, and crab. Olmecs and Mayans introduced corn, chiles, and herbs, and colonizing Spaniards brought Old World flavors to its New World abundance.

12 large prawns, peeled
1 pound medium-size scallops
5 tablespoons olive oil
5-6 cloves garlic
1 jalapeno, seeds removed and finely diced
2 cups chicken broth
2 12 oz. cans black beans, drained and rinsed
1 12 oz. cans white corn niblets, drained, optional
2 12 oz. can yellow corn niblets, drained
12 roma tomatoes, quartered
Fresh thyme leaves and fresh chopped chives

Serves 4

Warm the olive oil, garlic and jalapeno in a large frypan. Sauté the prawns and scallops for one to two minutes, until bright pink, and remove. In a six quart saucepot, combine the oil, garlic, and jalapeno mixture with the broth, beans, corn, and tomatoes.

Heat the chili through, and just before serving, add the seafood and fresh chopped herbs, cooking for an additional 3 to 5 minutes.

Serve with toasted baguettes, lightly brushed with olive oil and crushed garlic.

Wine suggestion:

Roussanne or another Rhône white, a little cooler than room temperature.

Three-Bean Chicken Chili

This dish features chicken sautéed with jalapenos, added to a brightly colored chili of black beans, kidney beans, and pink lentils, dressed with herbs and cilantro.

3-4 boneless, skinless chicken breasts
1/4 cup olive oil
5-6 garlic cloves, finely chopped
1 jalapeno, seeds removed, finely diced
3 tablespoons white Worcestershire sauce
1 12 oz. can red kidney beans, drained and rinsed
1 12 oz. can black beans, drained and rinsed
1 cup pink lentils, rinsed and soaked one hour
6 roma tomatoes, chopped
1 12 oz. can tomato sauce
1 bunch green onions, chopped
1 tablespoon each fresh tarragon, chives, oregano, and thyme, finely chopped
Sour cream and extra herbs for garnish, optional

Serves 4-6

Place the lentils in a small pan and cover with water. Boil for five minutes, turn off the heat, and allow to soak for one hour. Warm the olive oil in a large frypan over low heat. Add the garlic, jalapeno, and white Worcestershire sauce. Clean and dry the chicken breasts, then add to the olive oil. Sauté the chicken in this mixture over medium heat until crispy golden around the edges. Be careful not to overcook the chicken or burn the garlic. If things get a little too sizzly, just turn down the heat.

Remove the chicken and set aside to cool, but save the oil mixture. Drain the lentils. In a six-quart saucepot, combine the beans, lentils, tomatoes, tomato sauce, and sauté mixture.

When the chicken has cooled enough to handle, tear or cut it into bite-size chunks and add to the chili. Simmer on low heat until thoroughly hot, approximately 30 minutes. After 20 minutes, add the onions and herbs.

Garnish with a dollop of sour cream and fresh, chopped herbs. Serve with thick slices of peasant bread, corn bread, or baguettes.

Wine suggestion:

Sangiovese.

Chicken Soup with Ginger and Leeks

Both ginger and leeks stimulate appetite, and fresh lime juice provides a potent source of Vitamin C, so this soup is excellent for recovering from an illness, or restoring balance to the body. Shitake mushrooms are also very balancing.

6 cups chicken broth
4 boneless, skinless chicken breasts
2 tablespoons olive oil
4 garlic cloves, peeled and chopped
1 leek
1/2 fresh ginger root, peeled and grated
1 cup fresh shitake mushrooms, sliced into bite-sized chunks
1 lime
Sea salt and freshly ground black pepper

Serves 6

In a large saucepot, heat the chicken broth over low heat. Brown the chicken breasts and garlic in the olive oil over medium heat, until golden and fragrant. Remove the chicken and let it cool. Scoop out the garlic and add it to the broth.

Trim and thoroughly wash the leek, taking care to separate the outer leaves, since leeks are grown in sandy soil. Slice, and add to the broth. Add the ginger and shitake mushrooms.

Shred or slice the chicken and add to the broth. Heat over medium heat for 15-20 minutes. Do not allow to simmer ~ the idea is to simply keep the broth hot enough to extract flavor, without overcooking the chicken and mushrooms.

A few minutes before serving, add the juice of one lime and sea salt and pepper to taste.
Serve with freshly baked sourdough bread.

Wine suggestion:

Chardonnay or sangiovese.

Chicken Stuffed with Whole Lemons

This recipe is actually very easy to make, allowing the cook plenty of time to assemble a salad and pour a glass of wine. We like to use fresh garden produce and Meyer lemons for exceptional flavor. Allowing the chicken to steam under foil seals in its flavor and produces an exceptionally juicy chicken.

1 3-4 pound chicken
1 teaspoon coarse sea salt
1 tablespoon coarsely ground black pepper
2 lemons, preferably thin-skinned, sweet Meyer lemons
1 handful thyme sprigs
3 cloves garlic, peeled

Serves 4

Remove any organs packed in the chicken. Rinse the chicken inside and out and pat dry.

In a small bowl, combine the sea salt and pepper with grated zest from one lemon and one tablespoon of thyme leaves stripped from the stems. (If you are using thyme from your own garden, save the strongest stems and twigs for lacing the chicken closed.) Massage the salt mixture into the chicken, inside and out.

Cut a deep, lengthwise slit into the remaining lemon. Tuck several twigs of thyme into the lemon and insert it into the chicken, along with several more sprigs of thyme, reserving some for garnish. Lace or skewer the chicken closed and tuck the neck flap under, spearing it closed with another twig.

Place the chicken in an 8" x 11" glass baking dish or a large ceramic casserole dish. Broil at 500° on a low rack for 20-30 minutes, or rotisserie the chicken for about 40 minutes over medium-hot coals, with the lid off. (Closing the lid will crisp the chicken skin before the chicken is cooked through.)

Some like it hot!
Our friend Tim Haueter tucks small slices of garlic and jalapeno (or other hot chiles) into small slits under the skin before roasting. On a rotisserie, the rendering fat carries the chile flavor through the roasting chicken and gives the crispy, golden exterior a nice, piquant flavor.

Wine suggestion:

A mellow chardonnay—or for Tim's version, an icy cold beer.

Coq au Vin with Baby Root Vegetables

Coq au Vin is an easy, classic, versatile dish. My favorite version uses white wine, because it doesn't overwhelm the flavors of chicken, spring vegetables, and herbs, but you can also make it with red wine, and you can simmer it on the stove instead of oven-roasting.

1 2-3 pound cut up fryer chicken
¼ cup olive oil
2 cloves garlic, peeled and pressed
1 cup mirapoix (diced carrots, white onion and celery)
1 sweet white onion, peeled and cut into eighths
3-5 new red potatoes, cleaned and quartered
2 handfuls baby carrots, cleaned and trimmed
1 handful baby yellow beets, cleaned and halved, optional
Sprigs of fresh herbs (rosemary, bay, or tarragon), optional
2 cups white wine
1 cup chicken broth

Serves 2

Rinse the chicken pieces and pat dry. In a large frypan, warm the olive oil and garlic for 5 minutes, then sauté the chicken pieces over medium heat until golden brown. Remove the chicken for a moment, and sauté the mirapoix until fragrant and translucent.

In a heavy 2 quart baking dish, arrange the chicken pieces and place the vegetables over and around the chicken. Add the herbs, one cup of the wine, and ½ cup of broth.

Bake at 400° for 40 minutes, covered. Check after 20 minutes and add more wine or broth if needed.

Wine suggestion:

A silky chardonnay with lots of fruit and vineyard presence, light on oak.

Harvest Pizza

Color, flavor, and texture piled high on a cheesy pizza.

1 prepared 12" pizza crust
2 tablespoons olive oil
3 cloves garlic, peeled and chopped or pressed
1 teaspoon cornmeal
3 roma tomatoes, sliced
1/2 cup chopped, pre-cooked ham
1/2 cup fresh asparagus tips
1/2 cup fresh or grilled mid-season yellow corn
1/4 cup chopped red bell pepper
1/4 cup chopped mandarin orange bell pepper
1/2 cup fresh basil leaves
1 cup mozzarella cheese, grated

Serves 4

In a small bowl, combine the garlic and olive oil. Heat the oven to 425°, with a pizza stone inside.

Brush the pizza crust generously with the garlic-infused olive oil. Sprinkle the pizza stone with cornmeal, lay the pizza crust on top, and bake for 5 minutes, until the crust begins to sizzle.

Remove the crust and brush on the remaining olive oil and garlic. Arrange the tomatoes, ham, asparagus, yellow corn, peppers, and basil over the crust. Sprinkle mozzarella cheese over all. Bake for 12 minutes, or until the crust and cheese begin to brown. Remove and allow to cool until cheese is set. Serve immediately.

Wine suggestion:

Chardonnay, pinot noir, or sangiovese.

California Pizza

Bob Fielding sent us this recipe from Boulder, Colorado. "This recipe showcases two of my favorite California food products—ripe green olives and almonds. It is quick to prepare and works equally well as an appetizer or a main course," says Bob.

1 prepared 10 oz. pizza dough
1/2 cup fresh mozzarella, grated
1/4 cup fresh provolone, grated
1/2 cup California green ripe olives (about 20 large olives), sliced thickly
1 1/2 tablespoons Italian extra virgin olive oil
1/3 cup fresh mushrooms, thickly sliced
3 tablespoons California almonds, sliced
Freshly ground pepper, salt, lemon

Serves 2-4

Preheat the oven to 450°.

Unroll the pizza dough and roll out slightly on a well-floured board. The result-ing dough should be about 1/4" thick or less, and about 10 to 12 inches in size. Transfer to a baking sheet or pizza pan and pinch up the edges slightly with your fingers. Brush the dough with one tablespoon of olive oil. Cover with the grated cheeses. Add the olives, mushrooms and almonds. Salt lightly, pepper liberally. Sprinkle with fresh lemon juice and the remaining olive oil. Bake for 8-10 min-utes. The edges of the crust should be brown, and the cheese bubbling.

Wine suggestion:

Bob recommends viognier or chardonnay.

Pork Tenderloin and Basil Carnitas

We use fresh herbs, tomatoes, and peppers from our winery garden to make this easy and succulent dish during harvest season, when guests are many and time is limited.

1 1 1/2 pound pork tenderloin
1/2 cup olive oil
1/2 cup red wine
1/4 cup white Worcestershire sauce
Fresh garlic chives, bay leaves, thyme and oregano
2-3 cups fresh basil leaves
2 cups chopped vine-ripened tomatoes
1 cup chopped white onion
1 cup chopped yellow bell pepper
4 flour tortillas
Salsa

Serves 4

Place the pork tenderloin in a one gallon sealable bag with the olive oil, wine, white Worcestershire sauce and plenty of chopped fresh herbs. (Strip the tiny leaves off the thyme stems, and gently crush the bay leaves.)

Marinate for 2-3 hours. Grill the tenderloin over medium-hot coals until faintly pink inside, about 10-15 minutes on each side. You can also sear the tenderloin on the stove over medium heat, and then roast it at 400° for 10-15 minutes, or at 300° for 25-30 minutes. Check the tenderloin after 15 minutes, because pork cooks quickly. If you have a meat thermometer, interior temperature should be about 150°, and the center should be hot, yet still pink and juicy.

Chop the tenderloin into bite size chunks, and serve on warmed (but still soft) flour tortillas with fresh basil leaves, chopped tomatoes, chopped onion and peppers, and salsa.

Wine suggestion:

Pinot noir, sangiovese, or zinfandel.

Sweet Pepper and Chile Beef Bouillon

Old fashioned bouillon consommé, made with peppers and chiles for that New World zing.
We rely heavily on purchased broths, but nothing can compare with a homemade broth or consommé. If you plan to spend a day at home anyway, making homemade broth is easy. You can ignore it for hours at a time, and it makes the whole house smell delicious.

4 pounds small beef neck bones
2 pounds oxtails, optional
1/4 cup olive oil
Salt and coarsely ground pepper
1/2 bulb, or 10 cloves, garlic, peeled
1 bunch celery, cut into large pieces, about 4 inches long
4 large carrots, cut into large chunks
4 white onions, peeled and quartered
1 bunch parsley or cilantro
1 red bell pepper
1 poblano pepper
1 jalapeno pepper
1 Fresno red pepper, optional
2 cups water
1/2 cup white wine

Makes about 1 quart

Warm the olive oil in a large sauté pan over medium heat. Brown the bones and oxtails in batches, turning frequently. Place the browned bones and oxtails in a large roasting pan, sprinkle liberally with salt and coarsely ground pepper. Remove the sauté pan from heat and deglaze with a tablespoon of water, scraping up all the caramelized brown bits. Add the deglazed brownings to the roasting pan. If you don't have a large roaster, use two 9" by 13" glass baking dishes.

Add the garlic, celery, carrots, onions, and parsley. Cut all the peppers in half, remove the seeds, and slice the peppers into wide strips. Add to the roasting pan, with one cup of water.

Roast at 350° for 1 1/2 hours, turning the bones and vegetables once after 45 minutes, and adding more water if necessary to keep the vegetables from drying out.

After roasting, place all ingredients in an 8-qt. sauce pot with 2 quarts of water. Put 1/2 cup of white wine in the roasting pan and heat the pan on the stove. Stir and scrape all the browned bits from the roasting pan into the water and add to the sauce pot as well.

Simmer briskly for 1 1/2 to 2 hours. The vegies and herbs should form a "raft" on the surface which will sift out suspended particles, resulting in a clear and deeply colored broth. If you don't have time to watch it that closely, don't worry—the broth will be a little cloudy but intensely flavorful.

Remove from heat and discard all meat and vegetable solids. Place the pot, covered, in the refrigerator overnight. The next day, skim the fat off the top of the chilled broth. If you simmered patiently, the resulting bouillon will be a flavorful, jellied consommé with chile overtones.

Serve cold as a first course in the summertime, garnished with peeled, finely diced cucumber and fresh herbs, or use as a base for winter soups and risottos.

Prawn, Roma and Basil Linguine

So simple, so fresh.

6 tablespoons olive oil
2 garlic cloves, peeled and pressed
2 pounds large tiger prawns
4 roma tomatoes, chopped
1 handful fresh basil leaves, chopped
2 handfuls linguine
1/4 pound hard Parmesan cheese
Sea salt

Serves 2

In a large saucepot, bring two quarts of water to a boil. Add a pinch of salt and one tablespoon olive oil. Add the linguine and cook until al dente, about 10 minutes. Drain and toss.

In a large sauté pan, warm the remaining five tablespoons olive oil and the garlic. Peel and rinse the prawns, leave to drain in a colander. In a small bowl, combine the chopped tomatoes and basil. Drain away any juice from the tomatoes.

Add the prawns to the warm olive oil and garlic. Turn the heat up to medium and cook until the prawns are blush pink, but not done. Add the tomatoes and basil. Cook until the prawns are bright pink and the tomatoes are hot through.

To serve, place one serving of hot, drained linguine on a warmed plate. Top with the prawn, tomato, basil mixture, and be generous with the garlic-infused olive oil. Grate fresh Parmesan cheese over the pasta. Garnish with a fresh basil leaf.

Wine suggestion:

Viognier, chardonnay or pinot noir.

Pesto Chicken with Farfalle

Another dish from Ted and Nancy Commerdinger ~ fast, lightly spiced, and satisfying to the tummy and palate.

2 boneless, skinless chicken breasts, washed and diced into 1" or 2" pieces
2 tablespoons Trinidad seasoning (available from Penzey's Spices)
1 tablespoon freshly cracked black pepper
1/2 cup basil or arugula pesto (frozen from your summer herb garden)
1 package farfalle (bow tie pasta)
1 package frozen baby peas
Red pepper flakes, optional

Serves 2

Thaw frozen garden pesto gently in the microwave until just warm and oily. Prepare the chicken and place in a gallon resealable bag with Trinidad seasoning and cracked black pepper. Shake to coat.

Cook the pasta until al dente, 7 to 10 minutes. When the pasta is almost done, pan sear the chicken for about 3 minutes and set aside. Microwave the peas until hot, but still fresh and green. Drain any residual melted water. Drain pasta and immediately place in a large mixing bowl, adding the pesto, chicken, and peas. Toss gently with wooden paddles, plate and sprinkle with red pepper flakes.

Wine suggestion:

Viognier, chardonnay or pinot noir.

Bracciole

This is a Panico family recipe, handed down for generations, and one of Dan's favorites, especially when Mom cooks it. The actual family recipe is 'a little of this, a little of that,' so feel free to play with amounts and ingredients. Dan's recipe for bracciole is also featured in Margaret Smith's cookbook, "Companions at Table."

This recipe requires about an hour of preparation in mid-afternoon or early evening—then a long period of simmering in the fresh marinara. Perfect for a family event, when you want to have a hearty meal but not be tied to the kitchen in the evening.

Meat and pasta:

4 top round steaks (about 2 pounds), cut thin and tenderized
1/2 cup olive oil
4 cups rigatoni

Stuffing:

1/2 pound hot or mild Italian sausage
1/2 pound prosciutto, chopped
1/2 cup Reggiano Parmesan, grated
1/2 cup Romano, grated
1/4 cup seasoned Italian bread crumbs
2 cloves of garlic, chopped
1 tablespoon fresh Italian parsley, chopped
1 tablespoon fresh basil, chopped
1 tablespoon fresh oregano, chopped
1 teaspoon salt
1 teaspoon cracked pepper
Kitchen string

Marinara Sauce:

Drippings from browning the sausage and steak

1 cup Dover Canyon sangiovese
1 cup yellow onion, chopped
1/4 cup garlic, chopped
2 cups mushrooms, sliced
1/2 cup fresh basil, chopped
1/4 cup fresh oregano, chopped
2 bay leaves
1 teaspoon cracked black pepper
1 teaspoon salt
2 tablespoons brown sugar
28 oz. canned, diced tomatoes
28 oz. canned, crushed tomatoes

Serves 4

Remove the sausage from its casings and brown in a large sauté pan. Remove the sausage, but leave drippings in the pan. In a bowl, mix together all stuffing ingredients. Place 1/4 of the mixture onto each top round filet. Roll up each filet and tie with kitchen string at each end.

Heat 1/2 cup olive oil in the sauté pan with the sausage drippings. Add the bracciole (the stuffed filets) and brown. Save the combined drippings and remove the bracciole.

To make the marinara sauce, first add onions to the drippings and caramelize. Add all remaining ingredients except the tomatoes. Stir and simmer two minutes, then transfer to a large, 8-quart saucepot. Add the crushed and diced tomatoes and warm over medium heat. Add bracciole, cover, and simmer 1 1/2 hours. During the last half hour of simmering, remove the cover and reduce the sauce to desired thickness. Prepare the pasta.

Serve over a bed of rigatoni pasta, cooked al dente. Garnish with fresh basil leaves and fresh grated Reggiano Parmesan.

Wine suggestion:

Sangiovese, pinot noir, or an old vine zinfandel.

Fresh from the Garden

Guacamole Mui Caliente

Not for the faint of heart, "mui caliente" is Spanish for very, very hot!

12 avocados
6 roma tomatoes, chopped fine
1 jalapeno, seeds removed and diced
1 yellow Hungarian wax pepper, seeds removed and diced
1 bunch green onions, chopped
3 cloves garlic, peeled and pressed
3 tablespoons red wine vinegar
Juice of 1/2 lemon
1 tablespoon Tabasco sauce
1 tablespoon white Worcestershire sauce
1/4 teaspoon red pepper flakes
1 bunch cilantro (optional), chopped fine
Sea salt and coarsely ground black pepper
8-12 flour tortillas

Serves 6-12

The easiest way to prepare avocados for guacamole is to cut the avocado in half and squeeze the pit out. Scoop out the avocado meat and mash with a potato masher or large fork for a chunky texture, or process in a food blender for a pureed consistency. Combine all ingredients and mix well. Season to taste with sea salt and pepper.
Broil the flour tortillas until light brown and crispy. Break into pieces over a bowl and serve with the guacamole.

Wine suggestion:

Cold brews, or fruity, chilled whites with some body, like viognier and chardonnay.

Garden Guacamole

Chunky and fresh, with an unusual combination of colors and flavors.

12 avocados
1 jalapeno, seeds removed and diced
1 yellow Hungarian wax pepper, seeds removed and diced
6 cloves garlic, peeled and pressed
3 tablespoons red wine vinegar
Juice of 1 lemon
1 tablespoon white Worcestershire sauce
12 roma or heirloom tomatoes, seeds removed, diced
1 yellow bell pepper, seeds removed, diced
1 mandarin orange bell pepper, seeds removed, diced
1 large English cucumber, peeled, seeds removed, diced
1 bunch green onions, chopped
4-6 white French radishes, diced
1 bunch cilantro, stems removed, chopped fine
Sea salt and coarsely ground black pepper
8-12 flour tortillas

Serves 6-12

Cut the avocados in half and squeeze the pits out. Scoop out the avocado meat and mash with a potato masher or large fork for a chunky texture.
In a small bowl, combine the diced chiles, garlic, vinegar, lemon, and Worcestershire sauce. Allow the chiles and garlic to marinate in the acid for at least 15 minutes.
Prepare the other fresh vegetables and add to the avocados, combining gently so the guacamole retains a chunky texture. Add the chile-garlic mixture to the guacamole and combine well. Season to taste with sea salt and pepper.
Broil the flour tortillas until light brown and crispy. Break into pieces and serve with the guacamole.

Wine suggestion:

Cold brews, or fruity, chilled whites with some body, like viognier and chardonnay.

Warm Garlic and Garden Sauté

A bruschetta-like dish of sautéed garlic in olive oil, dressed with herbs, chopped peppers and tomatoes. We pour it liberally over pasta, rice, potatoes, and meats.

4-6 tablespoons extra virgin olive oil
3-4 cloves garlic, peeled and chopped
6 roma tomatoes, finely chopped
1 yellow bell pepper or 6" yellow crookneck squash, finely chopped
1 cup Italian brown mushrooms, finely chopped
1 teaspoon each finely chopped garlic chives, oregano, and thyme

Serves 2

In a large skillet, gently warm the olive oil and garlic over low heat. Add the pepper or squash, and the mushrooms, and sauté for 3 minutes, until tender and fragrant. Add the herbs and sauté another minute. Add the tomatoes last, turn up the heat to medium, and sauté just until the tomatoes are hot through.
Serve immediately over pasta, potatoes, or as a condiment with grilled meats.

Wine suggestion:

If serving as a main dish over pasta or potatoes, try a red with spicy, herbal notes and a delicious jamminess, like a deep sangiovese or old vine zinfandel.

Roasted Pepper Pesto

This condiment is delicious with steaks, tritip, potatoes, or simply spread over sliced baguettes as an hors d'oeuvre.

2 poblano chiles
2 jalapeno chiles
2 anaheim chiles
2 red bell peppers
1 yellow or orange bell pepper
5 cloves garlic, minced or pressed
5 tablespoons olive oil
1/4 cup pine nuts, lightly toasted

Serves 6

Place the chiles, peppers, and garlic on a lightly oiled cookie sheet and roast in a 400° oven until soft and browned. Turn vegetables so they brown evenly. (Or you can grill the peppers and chiles.) Remove stems, seeds, and burnt parts of skin. Place all ingredients in a food processor or blender and coarsely pulse until blended but still chunky.

Wine suggestion:

Grilling sweetens the hotter peppers, but this condiment may turn out a little differently every time you make it. If you're serving this on baguettes as a stand-alone appetizer, try sangiovese or pinot noir with a milder version, and a robust zinfandel when the chiles have more flavor.

Gorgonzola Potatoes

A rich, pungent variation on mashed potatoes, excellent with roasts and tritip.

8 to 10 new red potatoes
1 cup milk
1/4 cup butter or margarine
1 cup Gorgonzola cheese, crumbled or broken into large chunks
Sea salt and ground pepper

Serves 6

Quarter the potatoes and boil in a large stockpot for 20 minutes. Test with a fork—when the potatoes break apart easily and have a fluffy texture, remove from heat and drain.

While the potatoes are still very warm, add the milk and butter and mash thoroughly with a handheld electric mixer. When the potatoes are mashed and fluffy, add the Gorgonzola and stir with a large spoon until thoroughly blended. (The cheese tends to make mixer arms hard to clean.) Add sea salt and pepper to taste.

Wine suggestion:

You'll probably be serving these potatoes with a hearty cut of red meat or with lamb, and Gorgonzola is excellent with deep red wines, so reach for a really good cabernet or syrah.

Roasted Salsa

This salsa is smoky, easy to prepare, and great as a condiment with grilled tritip.

4 large cloves garlic
1 sweet white onion, like a Mayan or Walla Walla, peeled and cut into eighths
2 large, firm tomatoes, cut into thick slices or eighths
1 poblano chile, seeds removed and cut into wide strips
1 serrano chile, seeds removed and cut into wide strips
1 yellow bell pepper, seeds removed and cut into wide strips
1 fennel bulb, trimmed and cut into eighths, optional
1/4 cup olive oil
1/4 cup fresh cilantro, chopped, optional

Makes about 1 pint

Grill all vegetables in a grill basket over medium coals, brushing occasionally with olive oil, until lightly browned and tender. Remove any blackened parts and pulse in a blender or food processor, adding additional olive oil until blended but still chunky. Add the cilantro.

Wine suggestion:

The grilled flavors of garlic, sweet onions, and peppers make this a natural for zinfandel, whether you're serving the salsa as an appetizer or a condiment with meat. The grilled fennel also goes well with a robust syrah.

Triple Threat Mashed Potatoes

Ted Commerdinger is a very tall, very large guy, and an excellent cook. This translates into copious quantities of excellent food. Ted and Nancy help prepare family meals for the Hartenbergers of Midnight Cellars on chaotic wine festival weekends, after schlepping cases of wine all day themselves. This is their version of comfort potatoes.

2 pounds baby red potatoes, scrubbed with skins on
1/2 head garlic, broken down into cloves
1/2 sour cream or IMO
1/2 cup butter
4 oz. cream cheese
Freshly cracked black pepper

Serves 4 normally, or just Ted and Nancy

Boil potatoes for 15-20 minutes, until easily pierced with a fork. (Do not overcook, however—potatoes that are too soft lose that soul-satisfying palate texture.) Meanwhile, bake the garlic cloves for approximately 15 minutes, until soft and aromatic. Drain the potatoes, then add the garlic, sour cream, butter, and cream cheese. Let stand for 5 minutes covered, mash, add black pepper to taste, and serve.

Wine suggestion:

If you crave Triple Threat Mashed Potatoes, you need a cabernet, or better yet, a licorice-and-smoke zinfandel with big-man spice and alcohol.

Asparagus in White Truffle Oil
with Prosciutto Raffia

Truffle oil is exotic and strong. While it may seem expensive, a few drops will flavor an entire serving.

3 bunches thin, fresh asparagus spears
4 teaspoons white truffle oil
1/2 pound prosciutto, sliced very thin
Olive oil

Serves 6

Trim the asparagus stems by at least one third, leaving only the tender, green part of the spears. Blanch the spears in lightly salted, boiling water for two minutes, just until bright green, but not cooked. Drain and cool. Separate the spears into 6 bunches.

Shred the prosciutto into long, thready strips. Loosely "tie" each bunch of asparagus with shreds of prosciutto.

Wipe a non-stick cookie sheet lightly with olive oil. Place each asparagus "bundle" on the sheet, evenly spaced apart. The prosciutto can't really be relied on to hold the bundles together, so move them gently and rearrange prosciutto threads as necessary.

Just before serving, broil the asparagus bundles about 12 inches from a preheated broiler for about eight minutes, until the asparagus softens and the prosciutto begins to sizzle and curl.

Gently place each bundle on a small side plate, and drizzle each bundle with one teaspoon of white truffle oil.

Serve with fish or a lemon-chicken dish.

Wine suggestion:

A heavy, tropical white like viognier or roussanne, or a light red like pinot noir or sangiovese.

Bruschetta Baked Potatoes

A hearty, colorful version of baked potatoes, and a meal in itself.

4 large baking potatoes
1/4 cup olive oil
4 cloves garlic, minced or pressed
4 roma tomatoes, chopped
1 cup broccoli florets
1 yellow bell pepper, finely chopped
1/2 cup asparagus tips
1/4 cup fresh garlic chives, finely chopped
1/4 cup fresh tarragon leaves
Salt and pepper

Serves 4

Clean the potatoes and rub lightly with some olive oil. Pierce each potato in several places with a fork and bake for 40-45 minutes at 400°, until soft and baked through.
For a speedier version, microwave the potatoes on high for 5 minutes, and then bake for 15 minutes.

Warm olive oil in a large sauté pan over low heat. Add garlic and warm gently for 10 minutes while preparing the other vegetables. Add the broccoli, yellow pepper, and asparagus to the oil and cook over medium heat until bright. Add the tomatoes last and sauté just until hot through—overcooking the tomatoes releases too much juice and makes the bruschetta runny. Just before serving, cut the potatoes lengthwise across the top and squeeze the ends together to open the tops. Sprinkle with salt and pepper to taste. Spoon the olive oil, garlic, and vegetable mixture over each potato. Garnish with chopped chives and tarragon.

This mixture is also great over steaks, eggs, and toast.

Wine suggestion:

A sangiovese, pinot noir, or chardonnay.

Salsas and Sauces

Pacific Rim Barbecue Sauce

This tangy homemade sauce is great with grilled chicken.

14 oz. can tomato sauce
1/2 cup hoisin sauce
2 mandarin oranges (or 1 navel orange, or 1 Meyer lemon), juiced
1/4 cup brown sugar
2 tablespoons soy sauce
2 tablespoons fresh, grated ginger
6 cloves garlic, peeled and chopped fine or pressed
1 teaspoon ground dried chipotle powder

Makes about 1 1/2 cups

Combine all ingredients in a medium saucepan and simmer for about half an hour, until reduced and slightly thicker. The sauce will not be as thick as purchased barbecue sauces, but it's all flavor—and the citric acid and sugar also act as tenderizers, so your chicken will come off the grill hot and juicy.

Garlic Ginger Marinade

A Pan-Asian marinade for seafood, chicken, and roasts.

1/4 cup extra virgin olive oil
1/4 cup fresh squeezed orange juice
2 tablespoons balsamic vinegar, optional—good with red meats
2 tablespoons brown sugar
1/3 fresh ginger root, peeled and coarsely grated
2 garlic cloves, peeled and mashed with a garlic press
1 teaspoon Trinidad seasoning (available from Penzey's Spices)
1 tablespoon rum, optional (to quickly extract flavor)
1/2 teaspoon sea salt
1/2 teaspoon lemon pepper

Makes about 1 cup

Combine all ingredients in a small bowl and whisk thoroughly. Allow the marinade to stand in a covered container for at least one hour before using. (This gives the garlic, ginger, and spices time to permeate the olive oil mixture.)

Green Tomato Salsa

A fun and colorful way to use up those late-season green tomatoes still on the vine.

6-8 green tomatoes, chopped fine
2 ripe, red tomatoes, chopped fine
2 jalapeno or yellow Hungarian wax peppers, seeds removed, diced
3-4 cloves garlic, diced or pressed
1/4 cup olive oil
1 tablespoon balsamic vinegar
1 English or Armenian cucumber, peeled and diced
1 yellow bell pepper
2 tablespoons green hot sauce
1/4 cup cilantro, optional
2 tablespoons toasted sesame seeds, optional

Makes about 4 cups

Combine all ingredients in the order listed and allow to marinate for at least one hour, preferably overnight.
Serve as a salsa with freshly toasted flour tortillas, or as a condiment with fish or sausage.

Orange Salsa

Citrus salsa with a kick—great served as a condiment with fish.

2 navel oranges or 4 mandarin oranges
1 cucumber, peeled and diced
1 bunch green onions, chopped fine
2 yellow Hungarian wax peppers, seeds removed, finely diced
1 bunch cilantro, optional
1 teaspoon freshly pulverized cardamom seed
1 teaspoon Hawaiian pepper sauce

Makes about 2 cups

Peel the citrus fruits and scrape or peel away any white pith still adhering to the fruit. Chop into small pieces. Remove the cardamom seeds from their pods and pulverize; I use an old electric coffee grinder because it's smaller and more convenient than a food processor. Combine all ingredients in a bowl, cover, and allow to sit for at least an hour. If you make it earlier in the day, it will have a chile kick by dinnertime.

We like to use one of the many creative Hawaiian pepper sauces available, as they generally contain hot red chiles and other flavors like pineapple or mango. If you don't have any on hand, regular red chile oil will do.

Brunch Ideas

Garden Frittata

A simple and healthy way to prepare eggs with vegetables. Fast and easy, you can make breakfast or dinner versions.

8 eggs
2-3 pieces thick, country-sliced bacon
3-4 mushrooms
1 tomato, chopped
1 cup arugula or baby spinach
2 cups Mozzarella or hard Parmesan, grated
Salt and freshly ground black pepper to taste

Preheat the oven to 400°. Fry the bacon in a skillet until crisp and lightly browned. Drain on doubled paper towels until cool enough to handle, and break into bits. Discard most of the bacon grease, leaving only a slight residue on the pan and sauté the mushrooms until soft. Beat the eggs thoroughly in a small bowl, adding salt and pepper. Pour into a 12" non-stick ovenproof skillet. Add the tomato, arugula or spinach, mushrooms, bacon, and one cup of the cheese, reserving one cup for topping. Stir until well distributed. Cook over medium high heat until the bottom of the eggs begin to firm up. Lift the bottom occasionally with a spatula to allow uncooked eggs to settle and firm up. When the edges are firm but the center is still soft, transfer the pan to the oven and bake about 10 minutes, or until golden on top. Add a generous layer of the reserved Parmesan or Mozzarella and bake another 3-5 minutes, until cheese is melted and begins to bubble and brown. Be careful not to overcook or the frittata will taste dry—the eggs should still be fluffy and moist.

Once you get the hang of making a frittata, you can add your own favorite ingredients. Sausage, asparagus tips, basil, and caramelized onions are also excellent in frittatas.

Bloody Marias

This is a British Bloody with a New World twist of chiles and pickled corn. Our property is part of what was once the old Rancho de la Paso Robles. From our hilltop veranda we have a view of rolling hills and oak forests once populated by Spanish rancheros.

1 quart tomato juice
1 lime or lemon for juice
1 lemon, cut into 8 wedges for garnish
1 teaspoon white or dark Worcestershire sauce
6 pepperoncinis and 6 tablespoons pepperoncini juice
1 teaspoon creamed horseradish
1 teaspoon Tobasco or Pepper Plant seasoning
Salt and coarsely ground black peppercorns
6 celery ribs with leaves
6 pickled baby corns, rinsed and drained
6 pickled asparagus spears
Vodka to taste, optional

Serves 6

Halve the lime or lemon and squeeze the juice into the tomato juice. Add the Worcestershire sauce, pepperoncini juice, horseradish, and seasoning sauce and stir. Add salt and pepper to taste.
Serve in chilled 8 oz. glasses, garnished with a wedge of lemon, a celery rib, a pepperoncini, an ear of corn, and a spear of pickled asparagus.

Bruschetta on Shepherd's Toast

A quick sauté of garlic, peppers, and tomatoes over hearty, toasted bread.

1/4 cup extra virgin olive oil
4 cloves garlic, peeled and chopped
6 roma tomatoes, finely chopped
1 teaspoon each finely chopped garlic chives, oregano and thyme
4 slices crisp country-style bacon, crumbled
Shepherd's bread, focaccia, or pane rustico, sliced 1/2" thick
8 oz. crumbled blue cheese or Gorgonzola

Serves 2

In a large skillet, gently warm the olive oil and garlic over low heat. Add the tomatoes and herbs, and sauté for 3 minutes, until tender and fragrant. Add the bacon right before serving. Toast or broil the bread slices until lightly golden. Serve toast while hot, spoon bruschetta over, and top with crumbled blue cheese or Gorgonzola.

Breakfast Burritos

A variation on the taco bar ~ just serve up a plate of warm flour tortillas, some fresh-baked tortilla chips, and a variety of fillings. Guests can design their own "breakfast burrito."

12 flour tortillas
8 eggs
Salt and pepper to taste
8 slices country-style, thick sliced bacon
4 avocados, peeled, pitted and chopped
4 firm, fresh tomatoes, chopped
1 bunch green onions, chopped
8 oz. fresh Mozzarella or Cheddar cheese, grated
Mild salsa

Serves 6

Broil 4 tortillas 8-10" away from the broiler until crisp and golden on both sides. Place the crisp tortillas in a serving bowl and smash into wedges with your hand. The tortilla crisps are for scooping up loose tidbits and post-brunch snacking. Set the remaining tortillas aside to warm later.

Prepare the avocados, tomatoes, onions, and cheese and serve separately in small attractive bowls.

Fry the bacon in a non-stick pan until firm and crisp, remove, and set on doubled paper towels to dry. Break into bits and place in a small serving bowl. Discard the bacon grease, leaving a light residue in the pan for scrambling the eggs. Scramble the eggs with salt and pepper and fry over medium heat until plump but still moist, about 2 minutes. Serve in a warm, covered, ceramic or glass bowl.

Warm the tortillas under the broiler until just hot through. Place on a warm plate and cover. Leave the oven on for guests who want to assemble and heat their burritos so the cheese will melt. Have lots of thick paper napkins handy.

Jalapeno Bacon

1 pound thick sliced country bacon
1/4 teaspoon whole cardamom seed
1/3 cone Mexican brown sugar, coarsely grated
1 jalapeno, seeds removed and diced

Fry one slice of bacon to render some fat. To crush the cardamom seeds, open the green pods, remove the small tan seeds until you have 1/4 teaspoon, then crush lightly between two spoons. Don't worry if they're not completely crushed—they will soften in the bacon fat. Combine the cardamom seeds, sugar and diced jalapeno in a small bowl. Divide the pound of bacon into three batches, and toss one-third of the jalapeno mixture into the bacon fat and stir. Lay the sliced bacon closely together in the pan, and fry over medium-low heat until uniformly brown and slightly crisp. Remove the bacon, scooping all those flavorful, browned bits of jalapeno and cardamom onto the slices. Drain the bacon well when you remove it from the pan, and set it on a clean plate. Remove almost all the bacon fat from the pan, leaving only a teaspoon or so for the next batch. Add another one-third jalapeno mix and another third of the bacon, continuing until all the bacon is cooked.

Stuffed Apricots

6 fresh apricots, halved and pitted
1 cup crème fraiche
1 cup mixed berries
1/2 cup chopped hazelnuts

Place a spoonful of crème fraiche in the pocket of each apricot and top with fresh berries and a sprinkling of nuts. Yum.

Banana-Nut Crepes with Fresh Peaches and Crème Fraiche

A grown up version of kids' cereal, and so easy to make.

1 cup Post Banana-Nut cereal (to make 1/4 cup crumbs)
1/4 cup all purpose flour
1/2 cup milk
1/4 cup lukewarm water
2 eggs
1 1/2 tablespoons sugar
Pinch of salt
2 fresh peaches, pitted and chopped
1 cup crème fraiche
1/4 cup chopped hazelnuts or sliced almonds, optional

Toss one cup of cereal into a blender or food processor, and chop into fine crumbs. Put the crumbs in a resealable sandwich bag for future use, measuring 1/4 cup back into the blender. Add the flour, milk, water, eggs, sugar and salt, and puree. Stop once and stir crumbs up from the bottom to make sure it all mixes well. The mixture will look like thin pancake batter.

Heat a 12" non-stick frypan over medium heat until you can feel the heat when you hold your hand 3" away. Lift the pan in the air and pour in a 4" pancake of batter, then tilt and swirl the batter outward until it stops spreading. Replace the pan on the burner and cook until the batter bubbles and the edges shrink and brown. When the bottom looks uniformly tan, carefully lift the crepe around the edges with a spatula, and flip. Cook the other side until it has golden brown spots, and then slide the crepe onto a plate to cool. Repeat. (These crepes will be slightly thicker than traditional crepes.)

To assemble the crepes, lay one crepe on a plate, spoon chopped peaches in a line across the crepe, top with a thin stripe of crème fraiche, and roll the crepe up. Top with a dollop of crème fraiche and nuts.

Morning Margaritas

2 limes, juiced
1 navel orange, juiced
1 Meyer lemon, juiced
1/4 cup white sugar
1/2 cup crushed ice
1 lime, cut into 8 wedges
A scosh of Tequila, optional

Serves 2

Combine juice, sugar and ice in a blender and mix at high speed. Serve in chilled glasses and garnish with a wedge of lime.

Just Desserts

Choosing and Serving Late Harvest Wines

It's traditional to serve a late harvest red wine with a chocolate dessert, but serving a sweet wine with a sweet dessert can be sugar overload for many people, particularly after a hearty meal. I like to think outside cheesecake and chocolate, and let the dessert wine *be* the dessert.

We serve late harvest zinfandel with sesame-glazed walnuts, crispy cookies, or pungent cheeses like a good English Stilton. A delicate juxtaposition of flavor often enhances the wine, as well as the dessert plate itself, pairing sweet and interesting flavors in a well-crafted dessert wine with dry flavors in cheese or pastry—much like the interplay between a flaky pie crust and a sweet-tart berry filling.

Well-crafted dessert wines are difficult and challenging to make. Unless extreme care is used in the winemaking process, the heavy sugar and alcohol content of dessert wines will overwhelm the flavor of the grapes. A well-made dessert wine retains distinctive flavors and varietal character, and may be even more intensely flavorful than a dry dinner wine.

Dessert wines, particularly those labeled "late harvest," are made from extremely ripe grapes which have been allowed to hang on the vines long after the regular harvest season has ended. The grapes raisin a little, losing some moisture content and conversely developing strong sugars and concentrated flavors. Particularly in red dessert wines, grapes harvested with a heavy raisin content will have prune-like flavors, while grapes harvested at maximum sugar prior to raisining will retain exuberant fruit flavors.

After harvesting these late grapes, often at a sugar content of 30 degrees Brix or higher, the winemaker begins fermentation. When fermentation is allowed to proceed naturally, the high sugar content is converted by very hungry yeast cells into alcohol. But most yeasts cannot survive alcohol contents over 17%, so fermentation slows and gradually stops at around 17% alcohol, with natural sweetness still left in the wine.

However, in order to prevent flavor-to-alcohol imbalances, the winemaker might decide to fortify his dessert wine. The addition of distilled grape brandy kills the yeast by shocking the wine with a sudden addition of alcohol. The purpose of fortification is not to add extra alcohol to a dessert wine, but to stop the fermentation process at a point where the winemaker feels that flavor, sugar, and alcohol are in balance.

Protecting the delicate flavors of a white grape through its transition into a dessert wine can be particularly difficult. You may be familiar with muscat dessert wines—produced from a sweet muscat grape. A few muscat wines are superb, but many rely solely on sugar to woo their market share, and can be less than unremarkable. However, the ubiquitous white muscat grape has serious competition from tiny, rare productions of excellent dessert wines made from orange muscat or black muscat grapes. If you've been unimpressed by muscat wines in the past, don't be afraid to taste new offerings from wineries specializing in these varieties—you may be pleasantly surprised.

Ice wines, referred to in German as "eiswein," are produced from grapes picked so late in the season that they froze. The water content of the grapes turns into ice. Winemakers then gently press the grapes, releasing only concentrated nectar from the grapes, minus their normal water content, resulting in wines with incredible focus and delectable sweetness. The best eisweins have powerful aromas of ripe melon, orange, and jasmine, with perhaps hints of almond and vanilla.

Late harvest zinfandel is a popular dessert wine in our appellation, and indeed, the dark purple, peppery fruit of zinfandels often evolves into intense, dark dessert wines that retain lots of raspberry, plummy fruit. Quite a few late harvest zinfandels, however, tend to taste raisiny or pruney, a style which appeals to some, but I personally prefer late harvest wines with balanced flavors of ripe fruit and oak. You can also find late harvest or port-style merlots and cabernets.

There's a world full of amazing dessert wines out there, including vintage ports from Portugal, honey-like Trockenbeerenausleses from Germany, the Vin Santos of Italy—made from grapes dried on beds of straw, with flavors of toffee and honey—and Sauternes from France, a group that includes the world's most sought after and expensive wines, like those from Château d'Yquem.

If you're having a dinner party, a fabulous dessert wine makes an instant and impressive dessert course, as well as a great conversation piece. Winery sales staff, or the salespeople at your local fine wine shop can help you find a dessert wine that will coordinate with the rest of your menu and fit your budget.

Lemon Cheesecake with Mandarin Marbling and Chile-Mango Sauce

Cheesecake will never seem tame again.

1 pound cream cheese, room temperature
1 cup sugar, separated into 3/4 and 1/4 cups
5 large eggs, room temperature
1 sweet Meyer lemon
1 mandarin orange, tangerine or tangelo
3 tablespoons unsalted butter, cut into small pieces
Food coloring, red and yellow, optional
1/4 teaspoon vanilla extract

Crumb crust:

1 1/2 cups graham cracker crumbs
6 tablespoons butter, room temperature or slightly warm
2 tablespoons sugar, optional
1/2 teaspoon cinnamon, optional

Sauce:

1 ripe mango
1 jalapeno, seeds removed, diced

Serves 8

A cheesecake is really just a rich egg and cheese custard, not a cake. Cheesecake batter must be well mixed but not overbeaten. If too much air is beaten into a cheesecake batter, it will puff up like a soufflé and then collapse as it cools.

Warming the cream cheese first allows you to blend the ingredients thoroughly without overmixing or breaking down the cheese. It's also important not to over-cook the cheesecake. Bake at low temperatures and remove from the oven while still slightly soft in the center—the cheesecake will continue to firm up after it has been removed from the oven. Cool it slowly under a large inverted pot, in its own sauna, of sorts, to prevent cracking and drying out while cooling. Paying atten-tion to basic techniques for this cheese "custard" will result in a firm, creamy cheesecake every time.

In a medium saucepan, make the marbling first, so it has time to thicken and cool while you make the crust and begin the cheesecake. Whisk together 2 eggs and 1/4 cup of sugar, until the egg mixture is light in color, then add zest from the mandarin orange, juice of 1/2 mandarin orange, and the butter. Simmer over medium-low heat, stirring constantly to prevent the eggs from cooking on the bottom of the pan, until the butter is melted. (The mixture will still be liquid, but will thicken as the butter cools.) Cook for another two minutes. For addi-tional color, add one drop red food coloring and three drops yellow food color-ing, if desired. Let cool and refrigerate to thicken. (Keeps refrigerated for about one week.)

To assemble the crust, combine the crumb crust ingredients in a medium bowl, and fork until well blended—or pulse the ingredients in a food processor until blended and sticky. Lightly oil an 8" to 10" cake pan and pat the crumb mixture over the bottom and up the sides. Freeze or refrigerate for at least 20 minutes.

Bring the cream cheese, eggs, and lemon to room temperature and preheat the oven to 300°. In a medium mixing bowl, combine the cream cheese, 3/4 cup of sugar, zest from the lemon, 1/4 cup lemon juice, and the vanilla, blending for only 30 seconds or so. Beat in 3 eggs, one at a time, just until incorporated. Scrape the batter into the crust.
Drizzle the marbling sauce over the cheesecake, folding in lightly with a thin spoon or knife. Smooth the top and place the pan on a cookie sheet. Bake for 45-50 minutes—until the center just barely jiggles when the pan is tapped. Remove and cool under a large lid or pan.

In a food processor or blender, puree one ripe mango and the chopped jalapeno.

Serve each wedge of cheesecake topped with a drizzle of chili-mango sauce.

Wine suggestion:

A developed dessert white wine, with lightly caramelized flavors. Serve slightly chilled.

Fresh Dates stuffed with Cream Cheese and Raspberries

Fresh dates are softer and plumper than the dried version available in supermarkets. Check your local farmers' markets or ask your grocer.

12 fresh dates
1/2 cup cream cheese
12 fresh raspberries
1/4 cup late harvest zinfandel

Serves 4

Slice each date open lengthwise, leaving the ends closed, to form a small cup. Smooth a spoonful of cream cheese into each date. Top each date with a raspberry. Arrange the stuffed dates on a plate and drizzle with fine stripes of late harvest zinfandel. Serve as a finger food.

Wine suggestion:

Late harvest zinfandel or zinfandel port.

Peaches and Crème Fraiche in Phyllo Cups with Toasted Almonds

We created this simple dessert to go with a dessert viognier—the flavors of peach, pastry, and almond mirror the flavors of the dessert wine, and the crème fraiche keeps it light and tangy.

1 package frozen phyllo squares
1 tablespoon butter, melted
2 fresh peaches
1/2 cup crème fraiche
1/4 cup slivered almonds

Serves 8

Preheat oven to 400°.

Separate the phyllo sheets, unfold and gently cut each sheet into 8 pieces, or separate the squares if they are pre-cut, and gently fold and tuck one square into each cup of a large muffin tin. Baste lightly with melted butter and tuck another square on top of the first. Bake for 10-12 minutes, until firm and golden. Remove and allow to cool. In a small frypan, lightly toast the almonds over medium-high heat.

Put a small spoonful of crème fraiche in each phyllo cup, and then a spoonful of peaches. Resist the temptation to overload the pastry with filling—the pastry should add plenty of crunch and flavor to the dessert. Top with a dollop of crème fraiche and sprinkle with toasted almonds.

Wine suggestion:

A white late harvest wine, with tropical flavors and some youthful acidity.

Strawberry and Mint Tostadas

Light and easy to make, this is a refreshing dessert for warm summer evenings—and can even be hauled along on picnics.

1 package frozen phyllo squares
1 tablespoon butter, melted
1 cup small, fresh organic strawberries, sliced or chopped
1 cup ricotta cheese
2 tablespoons sugar
1/4 cup milk
1/4 cup fresh mint leaves, chopped fine, and extra leaves for garnish

Serves 4

Preheat oven to 400°.

Thaw and unfold the phyllo squares, and trim into circles. Baste one circle with melted butter, place another circle on top, and repeat until you have 3 layers. Bake on an ungreased cookie sheet at 400° for 10-12 minutes, until firm and golden. Remove from the oven and allow to cool.

Whip the ricotta cheese, sugar, and milk until well blended. Spread a small spoonful of the ricotta mixture over each pastry tostada. Spoon fresh strawberries on top, and sprinkle with chopped mint. Garnish with a mint leaf.

Wine suggestion:

A fruity Champagnois-style sparkler, or a frizzante moscato.

Parmesan-Pepper Cherry Pie

This recipe was inspired by my love of spicy, herbal cabernets. It's a simple connection—if you like cabernets with spice, grip, and flavors of bay and mint.

Crust:

2 cups all purpose flour
1/2 cup grated hard Parmesan
2 teaspoons coarsely ground black peppercorn
1/3 cup shortening
6 tablespoons butter (not margarine)
1/3 cup plus 1 tablespoon ice cold water

Preheat the oven to 400°.

Measure the shortening, butter, and water and place in the freezer for about 15 minutes. Assemble the filling while the crust ingredients chill. (Ice cold ingredients make it easier to process in a food processor.)

Put all crust ingredients except the water in a blender or food processor, and pulse until the mixture is a combination of fine and pea-sized crumbs. Drizzle half the cold water over and pulse until sticky. Remove to a mixing bowl, pour the rest of the water over, and mix by hand until the dough forms a clean ball. Roll it around a little to pick up the loose bits. (Do not over manipulate pie dough. It's not bread—beating it up will make it tough.) Separate the dough into 2 balls, one slightly larger than the other. Throw a handful of flour on a clean surface and pat the large ball into a patty. Put a little flour on top, and roll out with a rolling pin, working from the center out. Apply a handful of flour whenever things get sticky, and rub your rolling pin with flour if it's sticking to the dough. If the edges crack open, just pinch them together and keep rolling until your patty is slightly larger than an 8-9" pie pan. Slide the dough into the pan and press down.

Roll out the second ball.

Filling:

4 cups fresh or canned cherries
1/4 cup cherry juice
Sugar: 1/4 cup for canned sweet cherries in syrup
       3/4 cup for canned sour cherries in light syrup
       1 1/4 cup for canned sour cherries in water
       1 1/4 cup for fresh sweet or sour cherries
3 tablespoons cornstarch
1 tablespoon lemon juice
1/4 teaspoon almond extract
2 tablespoons butter, cut into small pieces
2 oz. Longhorn cheddar cheese, optional

Combine all ingredients except the butter and cheese, and let stand for at least 15 minutes.

When the crust is prepared, pour the pie filling in, dot with the butter, and place the top crust over. Roll the edges together and twist or crimp, tearing off excess dough until you have a nice edge. Cut slits in the top crust to let steam and juice escape. Place the pie in the oven as quickly as possible, so the juice doesn't soak through the bottom crust.

Bake at 400° for 30 minutes, to set the crust, then reduce the oven temperature to 325° and bake for another 25-35 minutes. The crust should be darkly golden and crisp, and juice should be bubbling up through the slits. Remove the pie and allow to cool slowly.

Wine suggestion:

Warm the pie and serve with a sliver of melted Longhorn cheddar cheese over the top, and a cabernet sauvignon.

Apple Pastry Wraps with Brie and Rose Petals

Large hybridized roses look great in the garden but their petals are often too thick and tough for cooking. Old-fashioned grandifloras are small and thorny, but small roses cover the bushes with cheeky abandon, and their tiny petals are translucent and delicate when cooked.

1/4 cup unsalted butter
1 package frozen phyllo squares or sheets
2 tablespoons butter, melted
4 Granny Smith or Gala apples, chopped
1 cup baby grandiflora rose petals (pink, rose and red)
Juice of 1/2 lemon
1 tablespoon ginger preserves
1 tablespoon clover or wildflower honey
1 teaspoon Chinese Five-spice (or 1/4 teaspoon each cinnamon, nutmeg, and cloves)
4 oz. Brie cheese
1 tablespoon butter, melted
1/4 cup toasted, sliced hazelnuts

Serves 4

Harvest 1/2 cup of loosely packed pink or red rose petals and rinse. If petals are large, cut off the white "pith" at the base of each petal. Keep the petals in cool water until ready to use.

Separate the phyllo sheets, unfold and gently cut each sheet into 8 or 9 pieces, or separate the squares if they are pre-cut. Baste one square with melted butter, place another square on top, and repeat until you have 2-3 layers, for 4 pastry wraps.

Warm the butter in a large sauté pan, and add the chopped apples, half of the rose petals, lemon, ginger preserves, honey, and spice. Sauté over low heat until fragrant and tender, about 5 minutes.

Preheat the oven to 400°. Place one spoonful of the apple mixture onto each square, and add a spoonful of Brie on top. Roll each square up and tuck the ends under. Place each wrap seam side down on a non-stick cookie sheet. Baste the wraps with melted butter and bake for 12-15 minutes, until the Brie is completely melted and the pastry is browned. Remove and allow to cool slightly.

While the wraps are baking, sauté the remaining rose petals in one tablespoon butter for about one second. Remove to a small condiment bowl to cool.

Garnish the wraps with a sprinkling of sautéed rose petals and hazelnuts.

Wine suggestion:

A sparkling muscat canelli or other white dessert wine, slightly chilled.

Easy Entertaining

The key to entertaining well and easily is to plan ahead. I have organized wine affairs for ten years, including intimate dinners for six, winemaker dinners for fifty, and open house hors d'oeuvres for hundreds. I also love impromptu dinners with family and friends, so I've refined my entertaining preparations to the following ten steps, and the most important is number ten—have fun.

Do a Walkthrough

The first step in pulling off a well-organized *affaire*, whether it's a simple dinner with friends or an elaborate wedding, is to do an imaginary walkthrough. Imagine you are the guest. Tick off on your fingers everything you would or would not enjoy as a guest, and plan every detail with your guests' comfort in mind, from the moment they enter the front door to bidding them good night.

If it's a mingling affair, set up comfortable centers of interest, and place appetizers in separate areas.

Sit in the Comfort Zone

Once your guests have arrived, will they be comfortable? Warmth, attention, and comfort are guaranteed to make a good impression, whether your event is casual or elegant. If you are seating your guests at a table, actually sit at the table yourself. Wiggle your elbows. Will you have room to sit down and get up without climbing over your neighbor? Will you be able to eat without bumping elbows? Can you talk to other guests without having to dodge tall candles and flower arrangements?

Create Special Touches—Quickly and Easily

If you want your event to look special, indulge in flower arrangements and candles, or pull out some old linens. Look around your own backyard, or turn to your local market for inexpensive centerpieces.

One of my favorite centerpieces is a simple arrangement of 3" clay pots holding variegated ivy, with 2" high candles sprinkled throughout the vines, interspersed with Bosc pears, variegated apples, and walnuts from our orchard.

A few swipes of gold leaf paint across the belly of a Bosc pear transforms it from market produce to art. For a harvest theme, you can swipe gold leaf on apples, Bosc pears, and walnuts; for Christmas mantels, use pomegranates and pine cones.

If you have a garden, plant small herb cuttings in clay pots for each table setting, with the guest's name written on it in metallic ink. At the end of dinner, pass around the metallic pens and let everyone add their signatures, so your guests can take home a living souvenir of the evening.

Herbs are a beautiful and fragrant way to decorate. Tie napkins with raffia and sprigs of bay and thyme, surround candles with small sprigs of herbs for a centerpiece, or place tiny sprigs in ice water or next to teacups.

Set up early

Give yourself lots of time—plan your party and menu at least a week ahead of time. Buy non-perishable groceries and supplies early in the week. That leaves you with just a quick dash to the store for perishables on the day of the party.

Clean house well ahead of time, so you're not tired, sweaty, and frantic the day of the party.

If you plan to assemble some last minute appetizers or serve hot foods like fondue, have all the chopping and grating done ahead of time, and the ingredients gathered in attractive small bowls.

Always set your personal deadline two hours in advance of your guests' arrival. There will always be a few things overlooked until the last minute, and having the extra margin gives you lots of time for some relaxed creativity and last minute fussing. You can pick some extra herbs and flowers for garnish, turn on the flowerbed sprinklers to provide a cooling spritz on a hot day, or just sit and relax with a tinkling, iced beverage.

Be ready for chaos

Throwing a party is like writing a novel. The characters take over and nothing turns out like you thought it would. Don't have too many preconceived notions about how the evening will go—relax and let your guests entertain themselves and each other.

Have a ready supply of attractive, clean dishtowels. When guests need a dish-towel—to clean up a spill, cover a dish, for an impromptu apron—you don't want to hand them a rag that looks as though you cleaned your barbecue with it.

Guests often want to help in the kitchen, and while it's fun to have everyone chopping, marinating, and peeling garlic, the kitchen table and counters quickly become covered with sticky debris, garlic peels, and vegetable ends. Another good use for new dishtowels—put one under each cutting board, and have your guests scrape their leavings onto the towel. When they're done, just pick up the towel and shake the leavings into a garbage can or compost recycling bag, leaving the kitchen clean and ready for the next project.

For a potluck event, set out a selection of extra serving platters, bowls, ladles and spoons. You'll be glad to have them handy in one place when everyone starts arriving at once.

Get Gophers

Delegating before and during the party makes the event more fun. Kids and teen-agers will often agree to help with a cleaning chore in exchange for "helping" with a cooking project. Youngsters love to help with party planning—it makes them feel adult and gives them confidence and pride when guests arrive.

Visiting relatives will often ask if they can bring something. Sometimes the secret message is that your relatives want to feel they're part of the event, and not just a guest. Think about what your relatives "specialize" in and ask them to bring something that gives them pride—like Grandma's fabulous shrimp dip, or a bot-tle of fine wine from Papa's cellar.

When the party begins, some people will feel nervous and awkward. By wel-coming them into your kitchen and giving them some simple prep chores, you'll help them feel like they're part of the action, and give them a way to break the ice with other guests.

Breathe and Smile

Whether you're a guy or gal, it's important to remember that this is your party. Give yourself a minimum of one half hour, uninterrupted, in which to do noth-ing but attend to your own personal grooming and sanity. Your smile and per-sonality will set the tone for the evening. Be relaxed, prepared, and ready to have fun.

Greet Everyone

Make eye contact with everyone as they walk in the door. Even if you're busy with something else, or talking to someone—at least give arriving guests a welcoming smile. Pay attention to your guests. Listen to them, look at their faces, and touch them.

Never interrupt or ignore your guests. If you're prepared, you can attend to last minute details and make your guests feel special at the same time. Never act as though details are more important to you than the people you've invited!

Work in Circles

Circulate and make sure no one is feeling left out or ignored. A good technique is to walk in clockwise circles around the room or house. Don't hurry—stop to visit with each guest and pick up platters that need refreshing, or sweep up a few crumbs. Make sure everyone has a beverage and feels comfortable. Be relaxed and warm, enjoy yourself and stop to chat whenever you feel like it—your guests can't relax if you're whizzing through the room like a summer tornado, snatching up plates of half-eaten food.

Relax and Have Fun

Your warmth and smile will set the tone for the whole evening If entertaining makes you nervous, then rely on the help of family, friends, or a good caterer. Let yourself enjoy your guests—it's the best gift you can give them, and yourself.

Sample Menu

Brie and Basil Crostini
Smoked Salmon Crostini
Pastry wedges with Nectarine~Ginger Relish
Piper Sonoma Brut

Asparagus with Prosciutto Raffia
in white truffle oil
1998 Dover Canyon sangiovese

Fresh Lobster
on a bed of baby mesclun, arugula and avocado
with olive oil, lemon and black pepper
2002 Dover Canyon viognier

Tuscan Pasta
served on a bed of rigatoni and fresh basil
1999 Dover Canyon Menage

White Chocolate Cheesecake
served with fresh raspberries and sesame~glazed walnuts
in a late harvest zinfandel and raspberry coulis
1997 Dover Canyon Late Harvest zinfandel

Sources

These are our favorite sources for specialty products, meats, herbs, and olive oil. We hope you'll check them out and try some of their products. We guarantee you'll be pleased.

A.G. Ferrari

> Italian cheeses, olive oils, balsamic vinegar, truffle oil, truffle-flavored rice, and other goodies.
> www.agferrari.com
> A.G. Ferrari Foods
> 14234 Catalina St.
> San Leandro, CA 94577
> Phone: 877-878-2783

Graber Olives

> Beautiful, luscious olives—big and meaty, with a nutty flavor.
> www.graberolives.com
> 315 East 4th Street
> Ontario, California
> Phone: 800-996-5483

Newport Meat Company

> High-quality cuts of meat, and our favorite source of lamb and duck. Currently available only by wholesale, so order through your favorite restaurateur.
> www.newportmeat.com
> 16691 Hale Avenue
> Irvine, CA 92606
> Phone: 949-474-4040
> Info@newportmeat.com

Ralph's Custom Meats

For locals and visitors-in-the-know, Ralph's offers Harris Ranch beef, Bernards pork, and specialty sausages out of a home-garage based business. They'll help you select a cut and share recipes and tips for roasting or grilling. Local wineries frequent Ralph's for their wine festival barbecues.
www.ralphsmeat.com
5400 Carrizo Rd.
Atascadero, CA 93422
Phone: 805-466-2114

Pasolivo Olive Oil

Locally-produced extra virgin olive oil from Willow Creek Olive Ranch. We serve this olive oil in our tasting room with fresh baked bread—it has an exceptionally spicy character, like puréed green olives.
They also produce a Lemon Olive Oil, infused with the zest of sweet Meyer lemons, and an Orange Oil. We use the infusions as finishing oils in sautés, as a last-minute brush on rotisserie chicken, or drizzled over steamed asparagus or artichokes.
www.willowcreekoliveranch.com
Willow Creek Olive Ranch
8530 Vineyard Drive
Paso Robles, CA 93446
Phone: 805.227.0186

Penzey's Spices

Our favorite source for spices—fresh, strong, and virgin. You have to try them to believe them.
www.penzeys.com
Brookfield, WI
Phone: 800-741-7787

Santa Barbara Olive Co.

The antipasto pillar of our winery—fresh and crunchy dilled baby corn, pickled asparagus and green beans, as well as an interesting selection of olives, including sun-dried black olives.
www.sbolive.com
12477 Calle Real

Santa Barbara, CA 93117
Phone: 805-562-1456

Sycamore Herb Farm

Fresh and dried herbs for culinary use, herb plants, grapevine cuttings, and cookbooks.
www.sycamorefarms.com
2485 Highway 46 West
Paso Robles, CA 93446
Phone: 805-238-5288

0-595-29958-X